All Color Book of
DELIGHTFUL
DESSERTS

All Color Book of
DELIGHTFUL DESSERTS

ARCO PUBLISHING INC.
New York

CONTENTS

Series editor: Mary Lambert

Published 1984 by
Arco Publishing, Inc.
215 Park Avenue South
New York, NY 10003

© Marshall Cavendish Books Limited 1984

**Library of Congress
Catalog Card Number: 84-70829**
ISBN 0-668-06215-0 cloth
ISBN 0-668-06221-5 paper

Printed in Italy

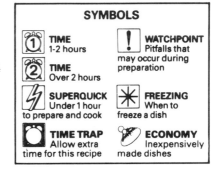

SYMBOLS

🕐 **TIME**
1-2 hours

🕑 **TIME**
Over 2 hours

⚡ **SUPERQUICK**
Under 1 hour
to prepare and cook

⏲ **TIME TRAP**
Allow extra
time for this recipe

❗ **WATCHPOINT**
Pitfalls that
may occur during
preparation

❄ **FREEZING**
When to
freeze a dish

ECONOMY
Inexpensively
made dishes

INTRODUCTION

A delicious dessert can be the ideal and fitting end to an enjoyable meal. This book contains a tantalising choice of different types of hot and cold desserts, some of which are fruity, others light and creamy and then the always popular ice creams and the more filling cakes, pies and flans. There are nearly 80 recipes and all have full color pictures and are ideal for the busy cook as they are easy to follow and quick to make. There is also a selection of extremely quick desserts for those occasions when time is really at a premium. The family's favorites are also included – those dishes like apple crumble and chocolate pudding that you are asked to make time and time again.

All the recipes contain cook's notes which give you serving and buying ideas for the dessert. They also tell you how many calories and how much time the dessert will take to make, plus giving alternative fillings to make the dish more economic or perhaps more exotic.

FRUITY DESSERTS

Pineapple bread

SERVES 4

4 medium eggs
3 tablespoons superfine sugar
1 can (13 oz) crushed pineapple
1 teaspoon ground allspice
6 tablespoons butter, melted
4 thick slices bread, crusts removed,
    cut into ½-inch cubes

TO DECORATE

4 rings canned pineapple
4 candied cherries

1 Put the eggs and sugar into a 1-quart ovenproof dish and beat lightly with a fork until the sugar has dissolved.

2 Stir in the crushed pineapple with its syrup, the allspice and butter. Fold in the bread cubes.

3 Press down the bread cubes lightly to level the surface, then cover the dish. Leave to soak in the refrigerator overnight.

4 The next day, when ready to cook, preheat the oven to 325°.

5 Uncover the dish and bake the dessert for 40-45 minutes or until the top is golden brown. Decorate the bread with pineapple rings and candied cherries.

Chilled cherry compote

SERVES 4

2 cans (1 lb each) pitted cherries, drained, with syrup reserved (see Buying guide)

2-inch piece stick cinnamon, or large pinch of ground cinnamon

2-inch strip lemon rind (see Cook's tips)

1 teaspoon lemon juice

about 2 tablespoons red currant jelly, or to taste

2 teaspoons arrowroot

2 tablespoons water

TO SERVE

4 tablespoons plain yogurt

8 ratafias (see Did you know)

1 Put the cherries into a large bowl and set aside.

2 Pour the reserved cherry syrup into a medium heavy-bottomed saucepan. Add the cinnamon, lemon rind and juice and 2 tablespoons red currant jelly. Stir over low heat to dissolve the jelly, then bring to a boil and simmer for 1 minute. Remove from the heat.

3 Blend the arrowroot with the water, then stir into the syrup. Return to the heat and bring to a boil, stirring. Simmer for 1-2 minutes, stirring constantly, until the syrup thickens slightly and is clear. Taste and stir in more red currant jelly to sweeten, if necessary.

4 Strain the syrup through a nylon strainer over the cherries. Mix well, then leave to cool. Cover and refrigerate the compote for 1-2 hours (see Cook's tips).

5 To serve: Spoon the cherries and syrup into 4 individual glass dishes. Top each with 1 tablespoon yogurt and 2 ratafias. (Stand the ratafias upright and at a slight angle, like butterfly wings.)

Cook's Notes

TIME
10 minutes preparation, plus cooling and chilling time.

BUYING GUIDE
It is worth paying extra for the canned cherries which are ready-pitted, not only because the cans contain more cherries, but also because pitting cherries is a tedious and often messy task.

COOK'S TIPS
Use a vegetable parer to pare a thin strip of rind from the lemon; this way you will remove only the outer colored part of the skin, not the bitter white pith underneath.

Remove the bowl of cherries from the refrigerator for about 5 minutes before serving to take the chill off the flavor.

VARIATION
This dessert can be served hot. Simply return the cherries and syrup to the pan and stir over low heat until the fruit is heated through.

SPECIAL OCCASION
Sprinkle the cherries with 4 teaspoons kirsch or cherry brandy before preparing the syrup. Use dairy sour or fresh heavy cream instead of yogurt.

STORAGE
Prepare up to the end of stage 4 and leave in the refrigerator for up to 48 hours.

DID YOU KNOW
Ratafias, tiny macaroons often used to decorate mousses, chiffons, ice cream and gelatins, are sold in boxes in good supermarkets and delicatessens. Their bittersweet almond flavor is particularly good with cherries. If you cannot obtain ratafias, hand around a plate of macaroons or other crisp almond cookies.

● 285 calories per portion

Spiced banana dumplings

MAKES 16
 1 package (17 oz) frozen puff pastry, thawed
 4 large firm bananas
1-2 tablespoons lemon juice
 1 cup superfine sugar
1 teaspoon ground allspice
1 egg, beaten

1 Preheat the oven to 425°. Brush a cookie sheet with water.
2 On a floured board, roll out sheets of pastry into rectangles, 20 × 10 inches. ! Trim the edges with a knife to straighten them. Let the pastry rest for 5-10 minutes, then cut into 16 squares about 5 inches each.
3 Cut each banana into quarters crosswise and toss in lemon juice to prevent discoloration. Place 1 banana quarter diagonally in the center of each pastry square. Mix the sugar and allspice, then sprinkle 1 teaspoon over each banana piece.
4 Brush the edges of 1 dough square with some of the beaten egg, then wrap the banana (see Preparation). Repeat for each dumpling.
5 Brush the dumplings with the remaining beaten egg and sprinkle over the remaining spiced sugar. Arrange the dumplings on the cookie sheet, then bake in the oven for 15-20 minutes or until the pastry is puffed up and golden brown.
6 Carefully lift the dumplings with a spatula. Serve warm.

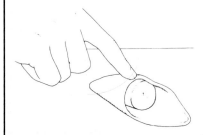
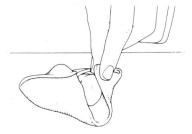
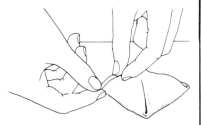

Oranges in Cointreau

SERVES 4

8 small oranges
½ cup superfine sugar
¼ cup water
¼ cup Cointreau (see Buying guide)

1 Using a small sharp knife, pare the rind from oranges, then cut the rind into shreds (see Cook's tip).

2 Put the sugar and water in a large heavy-bottomed saucepan. Stir over very low heat until the sugar has dissolved, then bring to a boil.

3 Add the orange shreds and boil for 1 minute, then remove with a slotted spoon and pat them dry on paper towels. Transfer to a saucer, cover and refrigerate until required. Leave syrup to cool.

4 Pare the oranges with a sharp knife, removing every scrap of white pith and taking care not to damage the orange flesh.

5 Cut the oranges across into thin slices, then stack the slices (see Preparation), to reshape each orange. Spear together with cocktail sticks and carefully transfer to a serving dish.

6 Add the Cointreau to the cooled syrup, then pour over the oranges. Refrigerate for at least 1 hour, spooning the juice over the oranges from time to time.

7 To serve: Sprinkle the oranges with the chilled shreds and serve at once.

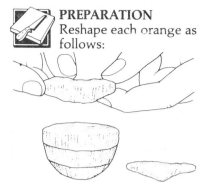

Mango spoon sweet

SERVES 4-6

2 ripe mangos, total weight about 1½ lb (see Preparation)

1 can (about 8 oz) pineapple rings in natural juice, drained with ½ cup juice reserved

¼ lb green grapes, halved and pitted

¼ lb black grapes, halved and pitted

1 Put the mangos in a blender with their juice and the measured pineapple juice. Work to a purée, then pour into a large bowl.

2 Cut each pineapple ring into 6 pieces and add to the mango purée together with the grapes. Cover and refrigerate for 30 minutes.

3 Spoon the mixture into 4-6 small dishes. Serve chilled.

Cook's Notes

TIME
Total preparation time (including chilling) is about 1 hour.

VARIATION
When fresh mangos are scarce, use 2 cans (about 1 lb each) mango slices, drained.

PREPARATION
Prepare each mango as follows:

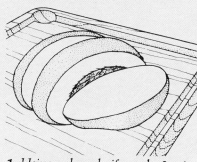

1 Using a sharp knife, make 2 cuts across the mango, each about ½ inch from the center, to make 3 sections. The middle section contains the large central pit.

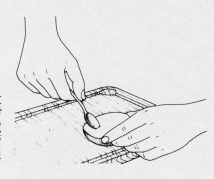

2 Using a teaspoon, scoop out the flesh from both side sections. Save any juice and add to flesh. Remove skin from central section then cut flesh from pit.

● 135 calories per portion

Plum and banana compote

SERVES 4

1 lb plums (see Buying guide)
1¼ cups water
⅓ cup sugar
¼ cup red wine or orange
    juice
2 small bananas
¼ cup flaked almonds

1 Wash and wipe the plums, then halve them and remove the pits (see Preparation).

2 Put the water and sugar into a heavy-bottomed saucepan and heat very gently until the sugar has dissolved, stirring occasionally. Bring the syrup slowly to a boil, without stirring, then boil for 2-3 minutes.

3 Carefully add the plums to the hot syrup; allow it to bubble up over them, then reduce the heat and cook the plums gently until they are just tender when pierced with a fine skewer. [!]

4 Using a slotted spoon, transfer the plums to a serving bowl.

5 Add the wine to the syrup and boil rapidly until thickened and reduced by about half. Remove from the heat and allow to cool for a few minutes, then pour over the plums. Leave until completely cold.

6 Just before serving, peel the bananas and cut diagonally into slices. Fold gently into the plums, then sprinkle the flaked almonds over the top. Serve at once or the bananas will discolor.

Cook's Notes

TIME
About 30 minutes preparation, plus a few hours cooling time.

BUYING GUIDE
Plums vary in size, color, juiciness, and flavor according to variety. Dark, purple-skinned plums are best for this dish, but you can use another variety if preferred. If the fruit is very large, cut it into quarters rather than halves.

When fresh plums are scarce or out of season, substitute frozen plums and thaw them before cooking. Alternatively, use drained, canned plums and do not cook them; use the syrup and boil it with the red wine.

PREPARATION
To pit plums, cut around them along the indentation from the stalk end, then twist the halves in opposite directions to separate them.

Ease out the pit with your fingers or the tip of a knife.

WATCHPOINT
Cooking time depends on the variety of plum used. It is important that the plums retain their shape for this dish, so take care not to overcook them or they will become mushy and the appearance of the dessert will be spoiled.

● 175 calories per portion

Harvest dessert

SERVES 4-6

½ lb plums, halved and pitted
1 lb cooking apples, pared, cored
  and sliced
1 cup sugar
½ pint fresh or frozen
  blackberries
1 sponge layer (½ package) cut into
  thin strips
softly whipped cream, to serve
  (optional)

1 Put the plums, apples and the sugar into a heavy-bottomed saucepan. Cover and cook gently for 10 minutes, stirring occasionally. Add the blackberries and remaining sugar, replace the lid and cook for a further 10 minutes, until all the fruit is very soft.

2 Turn the fruit into a strainer set over a bowl to drain off juice.

3 Arrange a few slices of sponge cake in the base of a 1½-quart pudding mold. Cover the sponge with a layer of fruit and sprinkle over about 1 tablespoon of the drained juice. Continue making layers in this way [!] until all the sponge and fruit are used, finishing with a layer of cake (see Economy).

4 Stand the basin on a plate, then cover pudding with plastic wrap. Put a small plate or lid which fits just inside the rim of the basin on top of the pudding. Weight the plate down, then leave the pudding in the refrigerator overnight.

5 To serve: Run a round-bladed knife around the sides of the dessert to loosen it, then invert a serving plate on top. Hold the plate and basin firmly and invert, giving a sharp shake halfway around. Carefully lift off the basin. Serve the dessert chilled, with cream, if liked.

TIME
40 minutes preparation, plus at least 8 hours chilling.

WATCHPOINT
Take care not to add too much juice: If the pudding is very soggy it will collapse when turned out on the serving plate.

ECONOMY
Do not throw the remaining juice away. It can be poured over the dessert after it has been turned out, or it can be kept in the refrigerator for 3-4 days and diluted with lemonade, cream soda or tonic water to make a delicious cold drink.

● 510 calories per portion

Gooseberry and apple amber

SERVES 4

- ½ pint gooseberries, topped and tailed if fresh, thawed if frozen
- ½ lb cooking apples, pared, quartered, cored and sliced
- 1 tablespoon water
- 2 tablespoons butter or margarine
- 2-4 tablespoons sugar
- ¼ cup fresh cake or bread crumbs (see Cook's tip)
- 2 eggs, separated
- ¼ teaspoon ground cloves or allspice
- ½ cup superfine sugar

1 Preheat the oven to 350°.

2 Put the gooseberries, apples, water and butter into a heavy-bottomed pan. Cover and cook over moderate heat for about 10 minutes, until tender. Remove from the heat and beat in the sugar to taste, the crumbs, egg yolks and cloves.

3 Turn the mixture into four 1-cup ramekins and level the surface. Stand the dishes on a cookie sheet and bake in the oven for about 15 minutes, until just set.

4 Meanwhile, in a clean, dry bowl beat the egg whites until standing in stiff peaks. Beat in the superfine sugar, 1 tablespoon at a time, beating the mixture thoroughly after each addition and continue beating until the meringue is stiff and glossy. Swirl or pipe the meringue over the gooseberry mixture in the ramekins.

5 Lower the heat to 275°; then return the dish to the oven for about 30 minutes, until the meringue is crisp on the outside and lightly browned. Serve hot or cold.

Cook's Notes

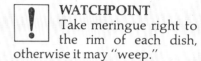

TIME
Preparation and cooking take about 1¼ hours.

VARIATIONS
For apple amber, omit the gooseberries and increase the apples to about 1 lb. Add the grated rind of 1 lemon with the cloves.

Use ground cinnamon or ground nutmeg instead of cloves.

COOK'S TIP
The crumbs absorb the fruit juices and prevent the mixture separating when the egg yolks are added.

WATCHPOINT
Take meringue right to the rim of each dish, otherwise it may "weep."

● 270 calories per portion

Fruit flambé

SERVES 6

1 can (about 1 lb) peach slices
1 can (about 1 lb) red cherries
1 can (about 14 oz) pear slices
1 can (about 8 oz) pineapple rings
¼ cup brandy or rum
¼ cup sweet butter (see Cook's tips)
¼ cup superfine sugar
1 teaspoon ground allspice
6 portions vanilla ice cream, to serve

1 Drain the fruits thoroughly, then blot dry on paper towels. Pit the cherries (see Preparation), and quarter the pineapple rings.
2 Pour the brandy into a cup and stand in a pan or bowl of hot water to warm through gently.
3 Melt the butter in a large, heavy-bottomed saucepan. Add the super-fine sugar and allspice and cook over low heat, stirring occasionally, until the sugar has dissolved. [!]

4 Add the fruit and turn carefully until evenly coated, (see Cook's tips), then cook gently to heat through.
5 Meanwhile, put the ice cream into 6 dessert bowls.
6 When the fruit is heated and all excess liquid has evaporated [!] turn off the heat. Pour the warmed brandy over the fruit and immediately set light to it. [!] Let the flames die completely, then spoon the fruit over the ice cream. Serve at once.

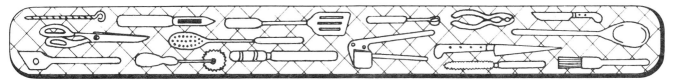

Gingered fruit cocktails

fruit mixture and sweeten with brown sugar, if necessary, ☒ then leave to cool.

2 Divide fruit mixture between 4 dessert glasses. Cover each glass

with plastic wrap and refrigerate for 20-30 minutes.

3 To serve: Spoon the dairy sour cream over the fruit and sprinkle the crushed cookies on top. ☒

SERVES 4

3 unpared dessert apples, cored and sliced

2 large oranges, pared and chopped, with pits removed (see Preparation)

½ small melon, pared, seeded and cubed (see Buying guide)

2 tablespoons light brown sugar (optional)

⅔ cup dairy sour cream

8-10 gingernut cookies, coarsely crushed

1 Place the prepared fruit in a heavy-bottomed saucepan. Cover and cook gently until the apples and melon are tender but not mushy. Remove from the heat. Taste the

Cook's Notes

TIME
25 minutes preparation, plus cooling and chilling time.

PREPARATION
Use a sharp knife to pare the oranges and take care to remove every scrap of bitter white pith.

BUYING GUIDE
Choose a cantaloupe or cranshaw melon for this dessert as they have very sweet orange-colored flesh, which is

highly scented. If either variety is unobtainable, use ½ small honeydew instead.

WATCHPOINTS
When you check for sweetness, remember that chilling will tone down the flavor and natural sweetness of the fruit mixture.

Serve the fruit cocktails as soon as they are assembled; if left to stand the cookies will become soggy.

● 255 calories per portion

Fruit kabobs

SERVES 4

6 tablespoons butter
¼ teaspoon cinnamon
¼ cup white wine, or 3 tablespoons water mixed with 1 tablespoon lemon juice
2 tablespoons honey
2 dessert apples
1 large or 2 small ripe dessert pears
2 small bananas
8 whole dates, pitted
8 maraschino cherries
4 slices bread, crusts removed

1 Beat ¼ cup butter with the cinnamon and set aside.

2 Put the remaining butter into a small saucepan. Add the wine and honey and stir over low heat until melted and blended. Bring slowly to a boil and cook for 1-2 minutes until the sauce is slightly syrupy. Remove from the heat and set aside.

3 Pare and core the apples and pear, then cut into chunky pieces. Peel the bananas and cut each across into 8 pieces. Thread the apples, pears, bananas, dates and the maraschino cherries alternately on to eight 6-inch long skewers (see Preparation).

4 Lay foil over the broiler rack and preheat broiler to moderate.

5 Place the skewers on the foil, brush liberally with some of the sauce, then place as far as possible away from the heat and broil for 10 minutes, turning them over frequently and basting with more sauce.

6 Remove the kabobs and foil from the broiler pan and keep warm.

7 Increase the heat of the broiler to high, then toast the bread on 1 side only. Spread the untoasted side with the cinnamon butter, then broil until crisp at the edges.

8 Meanwhile, reheat any remaining sauce until bubbling. Place the toast on individual serving plates and place 2 kabobs on each. Pour over the hot sauce and serve at once.

Cook's Notes

 TIME
These tasty kabobs take about 30 minutes to prepare and cook.

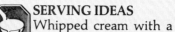 **SERVING IDEAS**
Whipped cream with a little sugar and liqueur added, if liked, can be served separately for "dunking" the fruit pieces.

Provide dessert forks and knives for eating. Use the prongs of the fork to slide the fruit off the skewers onto the hot toast.

PREPARATION
The apples and pears can be prepared up to 1 hour in advance and left to soak in the sauce to prevent them discoloring (Do not soak the bananas or they will become too soft to thread.)

If the apples have glossy unblemished skin, you can leave them unpared.

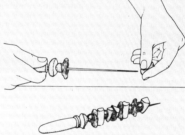

Threading alternate pieces of apple, pear and banana with whole dates and cherries.

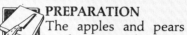 **VARIATIONS**
Use canned fruit instead of fresh, as long as it is firm and well drained. Peaches, apricots and pears are the most suitable. Cooked and drained dried fruit such as apples, apricots and prunes can also be used. Candied cherries can replace maraschino cherries.

Finely chopped walnuts may be mixed with the butter and cinnamon to spread on the untoasted side of the bread.

● 360 calories per portion

Coupe Jacques

SERVES 6

¾ lb mixed fresh fruits, cut into
   small pieces (see Cook's tips)
3 tablespoons kirsch or orange-
   flavored liqueur (see Economy)
sugar, to taste
1 pint lemon sherbet
1 pint strawberry sherbet

1 Place 6 shallow bowls in the refrigerator to chill.

2 Put the fruits into a bowl and sprinkle with 2 tablespoons of the liqueur and add sugar to taste. Mix gently but thoroughly, then cover and refrigerate for at least 1 hour.

3 To serve: Put 1 scoop or large spoonful each of lemon and strawberry sherbet side by side in each of the chilled bowls. Carefully drain off any excess juice from the mixed chilled fruits, then divide the fruits equally between the bowls, spooning them in between and on top of the 2 sherbets. Sprinkle over the remaining liqueur and serve at once.

Cook's Notes

 TIME
20-30 minutes preparation (depending on the fruits used), plus chilling time.

COOK'S TIP
You can use any combination of fruits. If using those which discolor when peeled (such as bananas or apples), turn the pieces in lemon juice before adding to the bowl.

ECONOMY
Use orange juice in place of the orange-flavored liqueur.

 DID YOU KNOW
This is a classic French fruit salad which is always served with kirsch and lemon and strawberry sherbets. What is not known about the dish is who the original Jacques was!

VARIATIONS
Other flavored sherbets, or water ices, can be used. If you find the sherbets difficult to obtain, use vanilla and strawberry ice cream instead.

● 220 calories per portion

Grilled pineapple

SERVES 4

1 large pineapple
4 tablespoons dark brown sugar
2 tablespoons butter
¼ cup rum

1 Preheat the broiler to high.
2 Cut the pineapple lengthwise into quarters, slicing through the green crown. Cut out the core and loosen the flesh (see Preparation). Wrap foil around each crown.
3 Arrange the pineapple quarters in the broiler pan. Sprinkle each quarter with 1 tablespoon sugar and dot with butter. Broil for 4-5 minutes until the pineapple is heated through. Transfer to warmed dishes and remove the foil.
4 Put the rum into a small saucepan, heat it through gently, then remove from the heat and immediately set light to it. As soon as the flames subside, pour the rum over the pineapple together with any juice from the broiler pan. Serve at once.

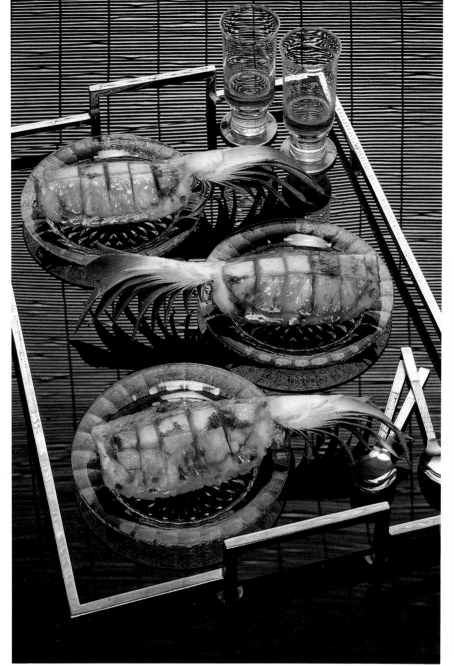

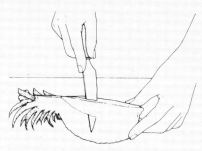
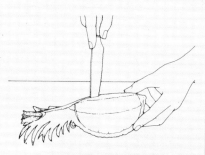

16

Date rice

SERVES 4

⅓ cup long grain rice
2 ½ cups milk
1 tablespoon butter or
   margarine
⅓ cup pressed dates, chopped (see
   Buying guide)
grated rind of 1 orange
melted butter, for greasing

1 Preheat the oven to 300°. Brush the inside of 1-quart ovenproof dish with melted butter.
2 Put the rice, milk and butter into a saucepan. Bring just to boiling point, then remove from the heat. Stir in the dates and orange rind. Pour into the prepared ovenproof dish and place the dish onto a cookie sheet.
3 Bake in oven for about 1 ½ hours, or until the rice is tender and most of the milk has been absorbed. Serve hot (see Serving ideas).

Cook's Notes

TIME
Preparation 20 minutes, cooking time 2 hours.

ECONOMY
If you are using the oven preheated to 325° for a main dish, the pudding may be baked on the bottom shelf.

VARIATIONS
Use other dried fruits, such as raisins or currants in place of some or all of the dates. For added flavor, sprinkle a little nutmeg over the top.

BUYING GUIDE
Buy dates that are already pitted – available from most supermarkets.

SERVING IDEAS
Serve hot, topped with chilled fresh orange segments, or drained canned mandarins.

COOK'S TIP
Heating the milk and rice first helps to keep baking time to a minimum.

● 220 calories per portion

CAKES, PIES AND FLANS

Ginger cream refrigerator cake

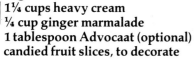

MAKES 8 SLICES

1 oblong ginger cake (see Buying guide)

1¼ cups heavy cream
¼ cup ginger marmalade
1 tablespoon Advocaat (optional)
candied fruit slices, to decorate

1 Remove the cake from its paper wrapper. Scrape off the remnants of cake sticking to the wrapper with a round-bladed knife, then crumble them between your fingers and reserve for decoration, if liked.
2 Cut the cake vertically into 4 equal slices, as shown in photograph.
3 Beat the cream until thick, then fold in the marmalade and Advocaat, if using. Sandwich the cake back together with about half of the cream mixture, then place on a narrow serving dish.

4 Spread the remaining cream mixture all over the cake to cover it completely.
5 Decorate the top with candied fruit slices and sprinkle with the reserved cake crumbs, if using. Refrigerate the cake for 1-2 hours before serving.

Cook's Notes

 TIME
20 minutes preparation, plus 1-2 hours chilling.

BUYING GUIDE
Choose a moist, oblong cake (sometimes sold as "Jamaica" cake).

FREEZING
Make the cake up to the end of stage 4, assembling it on a freezer tray. Open freeze until solid, then place carefully in a rigid container. Seal, label and store in the freezer for up to 3 months. To serve: Remove from container and place on a serving dish; thaw at room temperature for 3 hours, then decorate.

 VARIATIONS
Use an orange- or lemon-flavored cake and add orange or lemon jelly marmalade to the whipped cream. Drained mandarin segments or fresh orange slices can be used to decorate the top of the cake, if liked.

 DID YOU KNOW
Advocaat is a thick and creamy, yellow Dutch liqueur; it is based on brandy and thickened with egg yolks and sugar.

● 335 calories per slice

Chocolate éclairs

MAKES 8

1 package (4 oz) choux pastry mix
(see Buying guide)
1 cup tepid water
vegetable oil and flour, for cookie
sheet

FILLING AND ICING
⅔ cup heavy cream
2 drops vanilla
1 tablespoon superfine sugar
2 squares (2 oz) semi-sweet
chocolate, broken into pieces
knob of butter
2-3 tablespoons water
1 cup confectioners' sugar

Cook's Notes

 TIME
20 minutes preparation,
40 minutes baking, plus
cooling, filling and decorating.

 BUYING GUIDE
Packages of choux pastry mix are sold by some larger supermarket chains.

PREPARATION
Brush a large cookie sheet lightly with oil, then dust it with sifted flour. Using the handle of a wooden spoon, or a finger, mark 4-inch long lines on the cookie sheet, 1½ inches apart.

TO PIPE CHOUX PASTE

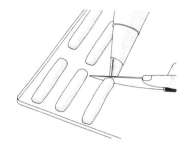

Holding the bag at an angle of 45° to the cookie sheet, pipe the paste along the guidelines. Raise the nozzle at the end of each line and cut off the paste cleanly.

● 280 calories per éclair

1 Preheat the oven to 400°. Prepare a large cookie sheet (see Preparation).
2 Put the pastry mix into a small bowl, add the water and beat with a rotary or hand-held electric mixer for 4 minutes. Put paste in pastry bag fitted with a ¾-inch plain nozzle, and pipe onto prepared cookie sheet (see Preparation).
3 Bake in the oven for 40 minutes, until puffed and golden. With a spatula, ease the éclairs off the cookie sheet and transfer to a wire rack. Split each one lengthwise in half with a sharp knife, then scrape out and discard any uncooked pastry from the inside with a teaspoon. Leave to cool completely.
4 Make the filling: Beat the cream until beginning to thicken, then add vanilla and superfine sugar and continue beating until thick but not stiff. Pipe or spoon the cream into the bottom half of each éclair, then replace the tops.

5 Put the chocolate, butter and 1 tablespoon water in a flameproof bowl set over a pan of hot water. Leave, stirring occasionally, until the chocolate has melted. Remove the bowl from the pan and beat in the sifted confectioners' sugar, a little at a time. If necessary, beat in 1-2 more tablespoons water to thin the icing.
6 Spoon or spread the icing over the tops of the éclairs, then leave in a cool place to set.

Cherry cream slices

MAKES 8 SLICES

2 sheets (1 17 oz package) frozen puff pastry, thawed

FILLING

1 can (about 1 lb) pitted black cherries in syrup
2 tablespoons cornstarch
2 tablespoons water
1¼ cups heavy cream
3 drops vanilla
2 tablespoons sugar

ICING

1½ cups confectioners' sugar, sifted
2-3 tablespoons warm water
1 square (1 oz) semi-sweet chocolate, melted

1 Preheat the oven to 450°. Dampen a large cookie sheet with water. Firmly roll out each sheet of puff pastry to a rectangle, about 14 × 6 inches. [!] Place on the prepared cookie sheet and prick well with a fork. Bake in the oven for 15 minutes, turning the pieces around halfway through the cooking time so that they become evenly browned. Transfer to a wire rack and leave to cool completely.

2 Meanwhile, make the filling:

Place the cherries, with their syrup, in a small saucepan and bring slowly to simmering point. Blend the cornstarch to a smooth paste with the water. Remove the pan from the heat and stir in the cornstarch mixture. Return to low heat and bring back to a boil, stirring constantly, then set aside to cool completely. [!]

3 Make the icing: Blend the confectioners' sugar with enough warm water to give a thick coating consistency.

4 Turn one layer of pastry over and spread the icing over the surface (see Cook's tips).

5 Beat the cream until it begins to thicken; add the vanilla and sugar. Continue beating until the cream stands in stiff peaks.

6 Assemble the dessert: Spread the cold cherry mixture over the other layer of pastry, then cover with the whipped cream.

7 Put the iced layer of pastry on top of the cream, iced side up, then lift onto a wooden board and place in the refrigerator for 30 minutes, or the freezer for 20 minutes.

8 With a sharp serrated knife, and a sawing motion, carefully cut the pastry into 6 slices. Using a teaspoon, drizzle melted chocolate over the top of each slice in a zig-zag pattern. Return to the refrigerator for 10 minutes to set before serving.

Frozen macaroon mold

SERVES 6-8

⅔ cup heavy cream
1 quart soft-scoop vanilla ice cream
   (see Buying guide)
¼ cup orange juice
¼ lb macaroons, crushed
¼ cup whole almonds, split and
   lightly toasted

SAUCE

¾ pint raspberries, thawed if
   frozen
¼ cup red currant jelly
1 teaspoon cornstarch
2 tablespoons water

1 Beat the cream until thick. Add the ice cream and orange juice and beat gently together until evenly combined. Quickly fold in the macaroons. Turn the mixture immediately into a 1½-quart freezerproof mold and level the surface. Cover tightly and freeze for at least 8 hours or overnight, until firm (see Cook's tip).

2 When the mixture is firm, make the sauce: Reserve some of the whole raspberries for decoration; sieve the remainder, then pour the purée into a saucepan and add the red currant jelly. Blend the cornstarch to a smooth paste with the water and stir into the pan. Bring slowly to a boil, stirring, and simmer for 2-3 minutes. Pour the sauce into a jug and cool. Cover and refrigerate. ✳

3 Turn the frozen mixture out of the mold onto a chilled, deep serving plate. ⚠ Pour the sauce over the dessert and spike with the almonds.

 **Cook's Notes**

TIME
20 minutes preparation (including turning out and decorating), plus at least 8 hours freezing.

 WATCHPOINT
When the dessert is turned out of the mold the mixture melts slightly, so have paper towels ready to mop up liquid from the base.

BUYING GUIDE
Use soft-scoop ice cream for this dessert, not the block variety which is too hard to blend in easily.

COOK'S TIP
You can make this dessert in the freezer compartment of the refrigerator. Turn the refrigerator to its coldest setting at least 1 hour

beforehand, and pour the ice cream and macaroon mixture into a well-chilled metal mold.

FREEZING
The ice cream and macaroon mixture can be stored in the freezer for up to 3 months. Freeze the sauce separately; thaw before use.

● 400 calories per portion

Mocha meringue

SERVES 8

3 large egg whites
¾ cup light brown sugar,
   sifted
1 teaspoon instant coffee powder
vegetable oil, for greasing

FILLING
4 squares (4 oz) semi-sweet
   chocolate, broken into squares
¼ cup water
1¼ cups heavy cream
2 teaspoons instant coffee powder
grated chocolate, to finish

1 Preheat the oven to 300°. Line 3 cookie sheets with non-stick parchment paper or waxed paper (see Cook's tips). Mark each piece with a 7-inch circle. If using waxed paper, lightly brush each circle with oil.

2 Put the egg whites into a dry, grease-free large bowl. Beat until stiff and white and standing in firm peaks.

3 Add the sugar, 1 tablespoon at a time, beating well after each addition so that the meringue is firm and glossy. Beat in the instant coffee powder.

4 Spread the meringue mixture evenly over the marked circles on the cookie sheet linings. Bake in the oven for 1½ hours or until crisp and dry in the center. Swap the top and bottom sheets after 45 minutes to insure even cooking. Set aside to cool, then peel off lining paper.

5 Prepare the filling: Put the chocolate and water into a small bowl over a pan of simmering water and heat until the chocolate has melted. Stir, then set aside to cool for about 10 minutes or until the chocolate begins to thicken.

6 Beat the cream until stiff, then put half of it into another bowl. Stir the chocolate mixture into one half and the instant coffee powder into the other half.

7 To finish: Put 1 meringue round onto a serving plate and spread it with half the coffee cream. ⚠ Cover with another meringue round and spread with half the chocolate cream. Cover with the third meringue round. Spread the remaining coffee cream over the top and mark decoratively with a fork.

8 Lightly beat the remaining chocolate cream until stiff. Put the cream into a pastry bag fitted with a small nozzle. Pipe 8 rosettes around the edge of the cake. Sprinkle the rosettes with a little grated chocolate. Serve as soon as possible, or within 2 hours if kept in the refrigerator, otherwise the mocha meringue will lose its fresh crisp appearance.

Cook's Notes

TIME
Preparation time 20 minutes, cooking time 1½ hours. Allow another 15 minutes for decoration.

COOK'S TIPS

If you do not have 3 cookie sheets, use large flan dishes, or put 2 meringue rounds on 1 large sheet.

If possible, use an electric mixer to beat the meringue.

WATCHPOINT
The cooked meringue is very brittle, so it must be handled with a great deal of care at this stage otherwise it may crack badly or break.

VARIATION

Stir ¼ lb thick fruit purée into the cream in place of the chocolate.

● 295 calories per portion

Chocolate cheesecake

SERVES 6-8

1¾ cups chocolate cookie crumbs
2 tablespoons sugar
6 tablespoons melted butter

FILLING
1 cup cottage cheese
½ lb cream cheese, softened
⅔ cup sugar
1 teaspoon vanilla
1 envelope unflavored gelatin
1 cup heavy cream
2 egg whites
1 bar (4 oz) cooking chocolate
1 tablespoon butter or margarine
2 tablespoons milk

1 Preheat oven to 350°. Mix crumbs, 2 tablespoons sugar and melted butter; press firmly onto bottom and up sides of greased 9-inch springform pan. Bake 10-12 minutes. Cool completely.
2 Whirl cottage cheese in blender until smooth; add cream cheese; blend until well combined. Pour into mixing bowl; stir in ⅔ cup sugar and vanilla.
3 Sprinkle gelatin over crean in small saucepan; place over low heat.

Cook's Notes

TIME
20 minutes preparation. Allow 30 minutes for chilling the cookie crust and 3 hours for the cheesecake filling to set.

FREEZING
Once the cheesecake has set, open freeze until solid, then remove from the pan and wrap in plastic wrap or foil. Store for up to 1 month. To serve, unwrap and then thaw overnight in the refrigerator. Decorate the top with fruit or chocolate just before serving.

WATCHPOINT
When swirling the chocolate into the cheese take the skewer right down to the bottom to give a marbled effect right through.

COOK'S TIP
To crush the bourbon cookies, put them whole into a strong plastic bag, and then roll them firmly with a rolling pin.

SERVING IDEAS
If liked, decorate the edge of the cheesecake with drained mandarin segments and dot with chocolate sprinkles or strands. Instead of fruit sprinkle coarsely grated chocolate around the edge.

● 635 calories per portion

Heat, stirring constantly, until gelatin is dissolved; cool. Blend into cheese mixture gradually.
4 Beat egg whites until stiff. Fold into cheese mixture. Refrigerate until mixture is thickened and mounds when dropped from a spoon.
5 Heat chocolate, butter and milk in small saucepan over low heat, stirring until smooth. then cool.

6 Measure 1 cup cheese mixture into separate bowl. Stir in melted chocolate mixture until blended.
7 Pour remaining cheese mixture over cheesecake; swirl with small flat-bladed knife to create marbled effect. Chill 4 hours until set.
8 To serve, run knife round edge of cake; remove side of pan carefully. Slide cake onto plate.

Spicy apple crunch

SERVES 4

1½ lb green apples (see Buying guide)

1 tablespoon light brown sugar
1 teaspoon cinnamon
2 tablespoons cold water
butter, for greasing

TOPPING
1 cup rolled oats
¼ cup light brown sugar
¼ cup whole wheat flour
¼ teaspoon salt
3 tablespoons butter or margarine, melted

1 Preheat the oven to 375°.
2 Grease a shallow 1¾-quart oven-proof dish thoroughly with butter (see Cook's tips). Pare, quarter and core the apples, then slice them thinly. Mix the sugar with the cinnamon. Layer the apple slices in the dish, sprinkling the spiced sugar mixture in between. Sprinkle over the water.
3 Make the topping: Mix the oats, sugar, flour and salt in a bowl. Stir in the melted butter with a knife until thoroughly mixed.
4 Sprinkle the topping evenly over the apples. Bake in the oven for 50-60 minutes, until the apples are very tender and the topping is crisp and browned. Serve hot or warm, straight from the dish.

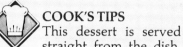

Cook's Notes

TIME
Preparation takes 20 minutes and baking 50-60 minutes.

SERVING IDEAS
This dessert is delicious served hot or warm with vanilla ice cream, chilled dairy sour cream or plain yogurt. It is also good cold.

VARIATIONS
You can use plain white flour instead of whole wheat flour, if preferred. Gooseberries (topped and tailed) or halved and pitted plums can replace the apples, but they will need an extra tablespoon of sugar; alternatively, you could use a mixture of apples and blackberries.

BUYING GUIDE
The best type of cooking apples to use are Winesaps, which reduce to a soft pulp when cooked.

COOK'S TIPS
This dessert is served straight from the dish, so choose an attractive one to bake it in. You can make the dish ahead and reheat it, if liked, in the oven at 325° for about 30 minutes.

● 335 calories per portion

24

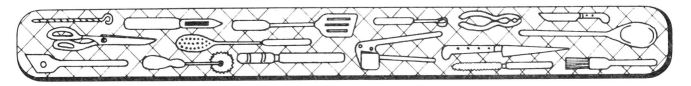

Redcurrant jelly tart

MAKES 10 SLICES
1 lb red currant jelly
⅔ cup butter, softened
⅔ cup superfine sugar
few drops of vanilla
1 egg, lightly beaten
⅔ cup ground almonds
1½ cups all-purpose flour, sifted
confectioners' sugar, for dredging
lightly whipped cream, to serve
extra softened butter, for greasing

1 Preheat the oven to 350°. Butter an 8-inch springform cake pan (see Cook's tips).
2 Beat the butter and superfine sugar together until very pale and fluffy, then beat in the vanilla. Add the egg, a little at a time, beating thoroughly after each addition. Using a wooden spoon, gradually work in the almonds and flour.

3 Draw the mixture into a ball with your fingers, turn out onto a lightly floured surface and knead briefly until smooth (see Cook's tips).
4 Reserve one-quarter of the dough in a cool place. With your hand, gently press the remaining dough over the base and 1½ inches of the way up the sides of the prepared pan. Neaten the edges.
5 Spread the jelly evenly in the pastry case.
6 On a lightly floured surface, roll out the reserved dough to a 8½ × 2 inch strip. Trim edges with a sharp knife, then cut lengthwise into 6 narrow strips.
7 Dampen the ends of the pastry strips, then arrange over the jelly in a lattice pattern. Press the ends against the pastry edge to seal, then flute the rim of the pastry. Bake in the oven for 45 minutes, or until pastry is cooked and browned.
8 Sift confectioners' sugar over the top of the hot tart, if liked. Leave to cool completely, then remove from the pan and transfer to a serving plate.

American chocolate pie
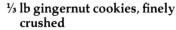

MAKES 6-8 SLICES

⅓ lb gingernut cookies, finely crushed

¼ cup butter or margarine, melted

butter or margarine, for greasing

FILLING AND TOPPING

1¼ cups milk

4 squares (4 oz) semi-sweet chocolate, broken into pieces

½ cup superfine sugar

3 tablespoons all-purpose flour

¼ cup butter or margarine

2 large egg yolks, lightly beaten

⅔ cup heavy cream

1 piece drained stem ginger, finely chopped, to decorate (optional)

1 Grease a 7-8 inch loose-based flan dish. Mix the finely crushed cookies with the melted butter until evenly coated.

2 Spoon the crumbs into the greased dish and press evenly over the base and up the sides with the back of a metal spoon (see Cook's tip). Cover and refrigerate for 30 minutes.

3 Meanwhile, make the chocolate filling: Put the milk and broken chocolate into a saucepan and heat gently, stirring frequently, until the chocolate has melted. ⚠ Remove from the heat.

4 Combine the sugar, flour, butter and beaten egg yolks in a bowl and mix together thoroughly with a fork. Stir in the hot chocolate milk, mixing well.

5 Return the mixture to the pan and bring slowly to a boil, stirring constantly. Reduce the heat and cook, still stirring, for about 5 minutes until the mixture is very thick and smooth.

6 Remove the pan from the heat and let the mixture cool for 5 minutes before pouring it into the cookie-lined dish. Leave for about 30 minutes until the chocolate filling is cold and set.

7 Carefully remove the pie from the dish and place on a serving plate. Beat the cream until thick, then spread over the chocolate filling. Decorate with the stem ginger, if liked. Refrigerate until required.

Nectarine tart

MAKES 6 SLICES
¼ lb cream cheese
   (see Cook's tip)
1 cup all-purpose flour, sifted
1 tablespoon superfine sugar

FILLING
4 nectarines
1¼ cups water
¼ cup sugar
1 tablespoon lemon juice
¼ cup red currant jelly or strained
   apricot jam, for glazing

1 Make the pastry: Beat the cream cheese with a wooden spoon until soft and smooth. Add the flour and sugar and continue beating until the mixture is evenly crumbly. Keep drawing the mixture together until it forms a soft dough.
2 Turn the dough out onto a lightly floured surface and knead briefly; wrap in plastic wrap and refrigerate for 1 hour (and up to 24 hours).
3 Preheat the oven to 400°.
4 On a lightly floured surface, roll out the pastry and use to line a loose-based, 8-inch fluted flan dish. Prick the base with a fork, then line with a large circle of waxed paper or foil and weight down with dried beans.
5 Bake in the oven for 10 minutes. Remove paper or foil and dried beans and return to the oven for a further 10-15 minutes until pastry is set and lightly colored. Remove the sides of the dish, slide the pastry case onto a wire rack and leave to cool completely.
6 Meanwhile, prepare the filling: Put the water into a heavy-bottomed saucepan with the sugar and lemon juice. Stir over low heat until the sugar has dissolved, then bring to a boil, without stirring, and simmer for 1-2 minutes.
7 Halve and pit the nectarines and lower into the syrup with a slotted spoon. Cover and poach gently for about 5 minutes until just tender. [!] Remove the pan from the heat. Lift nectarines out of the syrup with the slotted spoon and leave to cool completely. Reserve 1 tablespoon of syrup in the pan.

8 Assemble the tart: Place the pastry case on a serving plate. Peel nectarines, if liked, then cut into thick slices or leave the halves intact and arrange them carefully in the pastry case.

9 Add jelly or jam to reserved syrup and stir well over low heat until melted. Allow the glaze to cool until beginning to thicken, then brush over the nectarines. Leave to set before serving.

Cook's Notes

TIME
10-15 minutes, plus chilling the pastry, then 1¼ hours, plus setting.

WATCHPOINT
Do not overcook the nectarines: They must keep their shape or the whole look of the tart will be spoiled.

VARIATION
Firm peaches can be used instead. Do not use canned fruit for this recipe.

COOK'S TIP
Pastry made with cream cheese is richer and more crumbly than shortcrust. There are also fewer calories. It has a delicious flavor which goes beautifully with fresh nectarines, but plain pie crust can be used instead, if you prefer. When using ordinary shortcrust pastry, you will need ⅓ lb dough for an 8-inch fluted flan dish.

● 245 calories per slice

Raised plum pie

SERVES 6
1 package (11 oz) pie crust sticks,
prepared
milk and superfine sugar, for glazing

FILLING
1 tablespoon cornstarch
1 teaspoon cinnamon
¾ cup superfine sugar
1½ lb ripe plums (see Buying guide),
halved and pitted
pouring cream or custard, to serve

1 Preheat the oven to 375°.
2 On a lightly floured surface, roll out just under half of the pastry and use to line an 8-inch pie plate.
3 Place the cornstarch, cinnamon and sugar in a strong, large plastic bag, then add the plums and shake well until the fruit is coated with the sugar mixture.
4 Turn the plum and sugar mixture into the pastry-lined plate, mounding it slightly in the center. Brush the pastry edges with water.
5 On a lightly floured surface, roll out the remaining pastry to a 9½-inch circle and use to cover the pie. Brush the pastry lid with milk, then sprinkle with superfine sugar. Pierce the top with a skewer or fork to make a steam vent.
6 Bake in the oven for about 45 minutes, until the pastry is golden brown. Serve hot or warm.

Cook's Notes

TIME
Preparation takes 20-25 minutes; baking time is about 45 minutes.

VARIATION
Cherry plum pie: Use only ¾ lb plums and ⅓ cup superfine sugar; omit cinnamon and cornstarch and mix the sweetened plums with 1 can (about 14 oz) commercial cherry pie filling.

BUYING GUIDE
Damson plums are ideal for this recipe. Other ripe plums can be used, but they must be firm – soft plums do not make a good filling.

● 410 calories per portion

Raisin pie

MAKES 4-6 SLICES
1½ cups all-purpose flour
pinch of salt
2 tablespoons superfine sugar
6 tablespoons butter or margarine, diced
1 egg, beaten
a little milk, for brushing
superfine sugar, for sifting

FILLING
2 cups seedless raisins
grated rind and juice of 1 lemon
½ teaspoon cinnamon
¼ cup sugar
⅔ cup water
2 teaspoons cornstarch
2 teaspoons water

1 Sift the flour with the salt and sugar into a bowl. Add the diced butter and cut it into the flour until the mixture resembles fine bread crumbs. Add the beaten egg and mix to a stiff dough. Wrap in plastic wrap or foil and refrigerate.
2 Preheat the oven to 425°.
3 Prepare the filling: Put the raisins, lemon rind and juice, cinnamon, sugar and water into a saucepan and cook gently for 5 minutes. Mix the cornstarch to a smooth paste with the water, then stir into the raisin mixture. Bring to a boil, stirring all the time. Remove from the heat and leave to cool completely.
4 Cut off one-third of the pastry and set it aside. Roll out the remaining pastry and use to line an 8-inch loose-bottomed fluted flan dish or a flan ring set on a cookie sheet.
5 Spoon the cold raisin filling into the pastry-lined dish. [!] Roll out the reserved piece of pastry to a round large enough to cover the pie. Dampen the pastry rim with water, then place the pastry lid on top and press the edges together to seal. Brush the top of the pie with milk, then prick it with a fork. ✳
6 Bake the pie in the oven for 25-30 minutes. Remove the sides of the dish or the flan ring and return the pie to the oven for a further 5 minutes to brown the sides. Remove the pie from the oven and immediately sift over superfine sugar (see Serving ideas).

Cook's Notes

 TIME
40 minutes preparation, plus 30-35 minutes baking.

! WATCHPOINT
Make sure that the raisin filling is quite cold before it is put into the pastry-lined dish. If hot filling is put into raw pastry it will make the fat in the pastry melt and thus cause the pastry base to become soggy.

✳ FREEZING
Prepare the pie up to the end of stage 5. Open freeze, then remove from the dish, or ring, and wrap in foil. Return to the freezer and store for up to 3 months. To serve: Unwrap and replace in the flan dish or ring; bake from frozen, allowing an extra 10 minutes.

SERVING IDEAS
This pie can be served hot, warm or cold, with vanilla ice cream, custard, whipped cream or plain yogurt.

STORAGE
The pastry and filling can be prepared and stored separately in the refrigerator for 2-3 days.

● 650 calories per slice

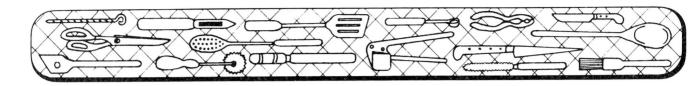

Frangipani tart

MAKES 6 SLICES

 1 sheet (½ 17 oz package) frozen puff pastry, thawed
 6 canned apricot halves, drained and finely chopped
½ teaspoon finely grated orange rind
½ cup soft tub margarine
½ cup superfine sugar
2 eggs, lightly beaten
1 cup ground almonds
melted butter, for greasing

ICING
½ cup confectioners' sugar, sifted
2 tablespoons orange juice, warmed

1 Preheat the oven to 375°. Lightly grease an 8-inch flan or cake pan with a loose base.
2 Roll out the pastry on a lightly floured surface and use to line the pan. Mix the apricots and orange rind together and sprinkle over the base of the pastry case.
3 Beat the margarine with the sugar until pale and fluffy. Beat in the eggs, a little at a time, then stir in the ground almonds. Spoon the mixture into the pastry case and level the surface.
4 Bake in the oven for about 40 minutes, until the filling is set and browned. Leave to cool in the pan for 10-15 minutes, remove from the pan and place on a serving dish.
5 Make the icing: Blend the confectioners' sugar and orange juice until smooth. Using a pastry brush, brush the icing over the top of the flan. Serve warm or cold.

Cook's Notes

TIME
The flan takes 1¼-1½ hours to make.

VARIATIONS
Omit the apricots and orange rind and spread 3 tablespoons apricot jam over the base of the pastry case. Add 2 tablespoons chopped blanched almonds to the filling.

 FREEZING
Cool completely, then remove from the pan. Do not ice. Wrap in a plastic bag, seal, label and freeze for up to 1 month.
To serve: Thaw in wrappings at room temperature for 4-5 hours. Warm through in a 375° oven for 15 minutes, then ice the tart.

DID YOU KNOW
This aromatic tart is named after the frangipani, a tropical plant noted for its fragrancy; its oils are used to make perfume.

● 505 calories per slice

Pineapple meringue pie

MAKES 6 SLICES

⅓ lb graham crackers, crushed

6 tablespoons butter, melted

FILLING

2 tablespoons cornstarch

2 tablespoons sugar

1 can (about 13 oz) crushed
    pineapple, well drained, with
    syrup reserved

¼ teaspoon vanilla

2 large eggs, separated

½ cup superfine sugar·

1 Mix the cracker crumbs with the melted butter. Spoon into a loose-based 8-inch cake or flan dish and press evenly and firmly over the base and up the sides. Cover and refrigerate for at least 30 minutes.

2 Preheat the oven to 400°.

3 Make the filling: In a small, heavy-bottomed saucepan, mix together the cornstarch and sugar. Stir in a little of the reserved pineapple syrup to make a smooth paste, then blend in the remainder. Bring gently to a boil, stirring constantly, then remove from the heat.

4 Allow mixture to cool slightly, then beat in vanilla and egg yolks. Stir in the crushed pineapple. Spoon the pineapple mixture into the cracker case and level the surface.

5 In a spotlessly clean, dry bowl, beat the egg whites until they stand in stiff peaks. Beat in the superfine sugar, 1 tablespoon at a time, and continue beating until the meringue is stiff and glossy.

6 Pipe swirls of meringue over pie or spread with a spatula, then draw up into peaks. Bake in the oven for 10-15 minutes, until the meringue is golden brown. Leave to cool completely, [!] then remove from the dish and place on a serving plate. Serve at room temperature.

Cook's Notes

TIME
30 minutes preparation, 10-15 minutes baking, plus at least 4 hours cooling.

WATCHPOINTS
Use eggs at room temperature.
Resist the temptation to remove the pie from the dish before it is completely cold as the cracker case may crumble.

STORAGE
The wafer case will keep for up to 2 days in the refrigerator. Wrap it well in foil or place in a plastic bag and seal tightly. The baked pie will keep fresh overnight if left loosely covered in a cool place, but not the refrigerator.

● 400 calories per slice

Citrus apple flan

SERVES 4

RICH PIECRUST PASTRY
1½ cups all-purpose flour
pinch of salt
½ cup butter or margarine
2 tablespoons water, chilled

FILLING
6 tablespoons butter or margarine
⅓ cup superfine sugar
2 cups fresh white bread crumbs
grated rind of 1 orange
½ teaspoon ground allspice
¼ cup thick-cut marmalade
2 green apples
confectioners' sugar, to dust

1 To make the pastry: Sift the flour and salt into a large bowl. Cut the butter into ½-inch cubes and add it slowly to the flour until the mixture resembles coarse crumbs. Sprinkle over the water, then draw the mixture together to a firm dough. Wrap in plastic wrap and refrigerate for at least 30 minutes before using.

2 Preheat the oven to 400°.

3 Roll out the pastry on a floured surface and use to line an 8-inch loose-based cake pan or a plain or fluted flan ring placed on a cookie sheet. Prick lightly in several places with a fork.

4 In a saucepan, melt the butter over low heat. Remove from the heat and stir in the sugar, bread crumbs, orange rind and allspice.

5 Spread the marmalade over the base of the flan. Pare, core and slice the apples and arrange over the marmalade. Spoon the bread crumb mixture evenly over the top and press down lightly.

6 Bake in the oven for 25 minutes, then reduce the heat to 350° and bake for a further 10-15 minutes until golden.

7 Remove from the pan (see Cook's tip), sift confectioners' sugar lightly and evenly over the top to dust and serve the flan hot.

Tropical flan

SERVES 6

10-inch sponge flan case
3 oranges
1 can (about 1 lb) pineapple rings in natural juice, drained with juice reserved
1 mango
1-2 tablespoons superfine sugar
2 teaspoons arrowroot (see Buying guide)
⅔ cup heavy whipping cream, to serve

1 Put the flan case on a flat serving dish.

2 Peel and slice the oranges over a bowl to reserve any juice. Remove any pits and the central pith and arrange around the edge of the sponge flan.

3 Cut the pineapple rings in half and arrange, overlapping, in a ring inside the ring of orange slices.

4 Again working over a bowl, score the skin of the mango lengthwise into several sections and remove the skin with a small sharp knife. Chop the mango flesh neatly and pile into the center of the flan. Squeeze the mango pit, which will have some flesh clinging to it, over the bowl to extract all the juice.

5 Strain the reserved orange, pineapple and mango juice into a measuring jug and make up to ⅔ cup with water. Stir in 1-2 tablespoons superfine sugar, to taste, and mix until dissolved.

6 Spoon ¼ cup of this juice over the sponge around the rim of the flan to moisten it.

7 Put the arrowroot into a bowl. Stir in a little of the fruit juice to make a smooth paste, then gradually stir in the remainder. Transfer to a small saucepan and bring to a boil over moderate heat, stirring constantly, until thick, smooth and clear.

8 Spoon the hot glaze over the fruit, allowing a little to run down the sides of the flan.

9 Leave in a cool place for 30 minutes, or up to 8 hours, then serve accompanied by the cream. (If liked the cream can be whipped until standing in soft peaks and piped around the edge instead.)

Cook's Notes

 TIME
Preparation takes about 30 minutes, but allow another 30 minutes for the flan to cool.

 BUYING GUIDE
Buy arrowroot powder at supermarkets and delicatessens. It looks like cornstarch, but has the advantage of giving a clear glaze when boiled, not a cloudy one.

 VARIATIONS
A sliced banana, tossed in lemon juice to prevent discoloration, can be used in place of the mango. Or use fresh or canned apricots.

● 375 calories per portion

Latticed gooseberry tart

SERVES 4

1 package (about 11 oz) pie crust sticks, prepared
little beaten egg, for glazing
superfine sugar, for dredging
custard or cream, to serve

FILLING
½ pint gooseberries, topped and tailed if fresh, thawed and well drained if frozen
2 tablespoons fresh white bread crumbs (see Cook's tips)
2 tablespoons sugar
½ teaspoon finely chopped fresh mint (optional)

1 Preheat the oven to 400°.
2 Cut off one-third of the pastry and reserve. On a lightly floured surface, roll out the remaining pastry and use to line a 9-inch pie plate.
3 Mix the gooseberries with the bread crumbs, sugar and mint, if using. Spoon into the pastry-lined pie plate and spread evenly. Brush the edges of the pastry with water.

4 Use the reserved pastry to make a lattice decoration over the tart (see Preparation). Brush the pastry lattice with beaten egg.
5 Bake the tart in the oven, just above the center, for 20 minutes; then lower the heat to 375° and bake for about 15 minutes more,

until the gooseberries are tender (see Cook's tips). Cover the top with waxed paper if the pastry is browning too quickly.
6 Remove the tart from the oven and sift superfine sugar thickly over the top. Serve hot, warm or cold, with custard or cream.

Cook's Notes

 TIME
30 minutes preparation, plus about 35 minutes baking.

 COOK'S TIPS
Bread crumbs absorb the juices produced by the filling during baking and help prevent the pastry becoming soggy.

Use a fine skewer to test that the gooseberries are tender.

 VARIATIONS
Fresh mint gives a pleasant flavor to gooseberries, but you could use a little grated orange or lemon rind, or ¼ teaspoon ground allspice instead.

 PREPARATION
A lattice is a very decorative way of topping a tart. If using a very soft or moist filling, make the lattice on waxed paper, then gently shake it onto the tart.

For a scalloped effect, the strips can be cut with a pastry lattice. A plain lattice is made as follows: Roll out the pastry to a rectangle, ½ inch larger than diameter of the pie plate. Cut in ½-inch wide strips. Place half the strips over the tart in parallel lines. Lay the remaining strips in parallel lines across the first set. Trim the edges and press to seal.

● 345 calories per portion

Mediterranean rice dessert

SERVES 4
1 can (about 1 lb) creamed rice milk pudding
1 tablespoon cornstarch
⅔ cup milk
2 tablespoons sugar
1 large egg yolk
grated rind of 1 small lemon
grated chocolate, to decorate

1 Turn the creamed rice into a saucepan and set over low heat.
2 Blend the cornstarch with 2-3 tablespoons of milk, then stir in half the remaining milk. Add the cornstarch mixture to the rice together with the sugar. Bring slowly to a boil, stirring, and simmer for 2 minutes.
3 Beat the egg yolk with the remaining milk, then stir into the rice pudding. Add the lemon rind and simmer, stirring, for 2 minutes more.
4 Remove the pan from the heat and pour the pudding into 4 individual dessert bowls. Sprinkle a little grated chocolate over each pudding. Serve hot or chilled.

Cook's Notes

TIME
Preparation and cooking take about 10 minutes. Remember to allow chilling time if serving cold.

ECONOMY
This is a quick and easy way to stretch a can of rice pudding to serve 4.

DID YOU KNOW
This type of pudding is popular in the Mediterranean, where it is often sprinkled with cinnamon.

● 185 calories per portion

Coffee mousse

SERVES 6

4 teaspoons instant coffee
¼ cup superfine sugar
3 tablespoons boiling water
1 envelope unflavored gelatin
3 tablespoons cold water
1¼ cups heavy cream
2 egg whites
small chocolate curls or chopped
    walnuts to decorate (see
    Preparation)

1 Dissolve the coffee and superfine sugar in the boiling water.
2 Sprinkle the gelatin over the cold water in a small flameproof bowl and leave to soak for 5 minutes, then stand the bowl in a pan of gently simmering water for 1-2 minutes until the gelatin has completely dissolved, stirring occasionally.
3 Pour the coffee into the gelatin liquid, stirring well to mix. Remove the bowl from the pan and leave the coffee mixture until tepid. [!]
4 Meanwhile, beat the cream until standing in soft peaks. Just before the coffee mixture is ready, beat the egg whites until stiff in a clean, dry bowl and using clean beaters.
5 Using a large metal spoon, quickly blend the coffee mixture into the cream, then fold in the egg whites. Divide the mixture equally between 6 small dishes. Cover and refrigerate for 2-3 hours, until set.
6 Just before serving, decorate each mousse with chocolate curls.

Cook's Notes

TIME
15 minutes preparation plus 2-3 hours chilling.

WATCHPOINT
You need to keep a close watch on the coffee mixture as it cools very quickly. Test the mixture frequently with a clean finger; it should feel just warm. Do not let it become too cool or it will set in threads as soon as it comes into contact with the whipped cream.

● 280 calories per mousse

PREPARATION
For a 2-tone effect, make curls from bars of white and milk chocolate.

Draw a swivel vegetable parer towards you, along the side of bar, to shave off small curls.

Rhubarb and orange cream

SERVES 4

1 can (about 1¼ lb) rhubarb
finely grated rind and juice of 1
**   orange**
1 tablespoon superfine sugar,
**   or to taste**
3 eggs
⅔ cup heavy whipping
**   cream**
sweet cookies, to serve

1 Put the rhubarb and 2 table-spoons juice from the can into a blender with the orange rind and juice and sugar. Blend at high speed until a smooth purée.

2 Beat the eggs together thoroughly in a flameproof bowl, then beat in the rhubarb purée.

3 Place the bowl over a saucepan of simmering water and cook for 10-15 minutes, beating constantly with a wire whisk until the mixture is thick and creamy. |!|

4 Remove the bowl from the heat, leave to cool, then chill in the refrigerator until absolutely cold. |!|

5 Beat the cream until it stands in soft peaks, then fold into the cooled rhubarb mixture. Cover and chill in the refrigerator for at least 6 hours (preferably overnight) before serving.

6 Serve chilled in individual dishes or glasses, with sweet cookies.

Cook's Notes

TIME
1 hour 25 minutes, plus at least 6 hours chilling.

VARIATIONS
Use fresh rhubarb when in season. Weigh 1 lb, trim and slice, then cook with sugar to taste until tender. Drain, reserving 2 tablespoons of the juice.

Try using canned plums instead of rhubarb, but strain them after puréeing to remove the skins. Add a pinch of ground cinnamon to give a deliciously different flavor.

COOK'S TIPS
If you do not have a blender simply mash the rhubarb thoroughly until it is a smooth, creamy pulp.

Use the finest part of the grater to grate the orange rind. Do not grate for too long in one place, but simply take off the rind, or the orange-colored part of the skin, because the pith underneath is rather bitter.

! WATCHPOINT
It is important the bowl containing the eggs and rhubarb purée should not come in contact with the water simmering in the pan. It should rest just above the surface of the water so the mixture does not boil and curdle or separate.

The cooked mixture must be quite cold before you add the cream, or the cream will flop.

SERVING IDEAS
This dessert has a soft, creamy consistency which is complemented by crisp cookies such as *langues de chat* or sponge fingers.

● 250 calories per portion

Fruit mallow

3 Spoon the mixture into 6 tall glasses. Cover each with plastic wrap and refrigerate for at least 8 hours, or overnight, to allow the flavors to blend and the texture to firm.

4 Remove the desserts from the fridge 15 minutes before serving to take chill off. Just before serving, decorate with marshmallows and wafers if liked.

SERVES 6

6 oz pink and white marshmallows (see Buying guide)
1 can (about 14 oz) fruit cocktail, well drained
1¼ cups heavy cream
2 tablespoons milk
extra marshmallows and fan wafers, to decorate (optional)

1 Snip the marshmallows into pieces (see Preparation) and put into a large bowl. Using a wooden spoon, gently stir in the fruit cocktail and mix until evenly blended.

2 In a separate bowl, beat the cream with the milk until standing in stiff peaks. Using a large metal spoon, fold the cream into the fruit and marshmallow mixture.

Cook's Notes

 TIME
Preparation takes only 15 minutes, but allow at least 8 hours chilling time. Decorating the desserts takes a few extra minutes.

BUYING GUIDE
Some supermarkets sell their own brand of marshmallow in 6 oz packages. They are also available in ¼ lb packages; in which case, buy 2 packages and use the extra to decorate the desserts. Tiny marshmallows are also available.

● 290 calories per portion

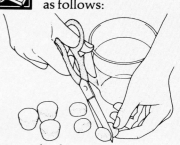 **PREPARATION**
Cut the marshmallows as follows:

Using kitchen scissors, cut each marshmallow in half across, then cut each half into 3 pieces. Dip the scissors into hot water at frequent intervals — this will prevent the blades becoming too sticky.

Apple flummery

SERVES 4

2 large eggs, separated
¼ cup sugar
2½ cups milk
2 tablespoons semolina
pinch of salt
1 large green apple, weighing about
  ¾ lb, pared, cored and puréed
juice of ½ small lemon

TO SERVE
1 red-skinned dessert apple
few drops of lemon juice

1 Put the egg yolks and sugar in a bowl and beat together until creamy.

2 Put the milk into a large saucepan and warm it over moderate heat. Sprinkle in the semolina and bring to a boil, stirring. Add the salt and lower the heat, then simmer for 10 minutes, stirring constantly.

3 Gradually stir in the egg yolk and sugar mixture until well mixed, then continue cooking very gently for a further 2 minutes, stirring all the time. Do not allow the mixture to boil or it will stick to the bottom of the pan and may burn.

4 Remove the pan from the heat, then stir in the apple purée and lemon juice until well blended.

5 Beat the egg whites until stiff and fold into the mixture in the pan, using a metal spoon.

6 Carefully spoon the mixture into individual glasses and leave to cool for about 30 minutes.

7 To serve: Thinly slice the apple, discarding the core, but leaving the skin on. Sprinkle immediately with lemon juice to prevent discoloration. Place a few slices on each serving and serve at once.

Cook's Notes

 TIME
About 50 minutes, including 15 minutes to prepare and purée the apple.

 COOK'S TIP
The flummery is a particularly light and refreshing dessert — it separates slightly into a shallow layer of liquid at the bottom, topped with a fluffy mixture.

? **DID YOU KNOW**
According to the dictionary, flummery is an old Welsh word of unknown derivation, but it refers to a traditional sweet dish (popular in the British Isles) which is milk and egg-based and always eaten cold.

● 250 calories per portion

Honeyed apricot whips

SERVES 4

¾ cup dried apricots
1¼ cups hot water
2 tablespoons honey
1¼ cups plain yogurt
2 egg whites
boudoir wafers, or chocolate fingers, to serve

1 Put the apricots in a small bowl with the hot water and leave to soak for at least 4 hours or, if possible, overnight.
2 Turn the apricots and water into a heavy-bottomed saucepan. Add the honey, cover and simmer very gently for about 20 minutes, until the apricots are tender. Remove from the heat and leave to cool completely.
3 Purée the apricots with the cooking syrup and yogurt in a blender. Alternatively, press the apricots through a strainer, then stir in the cooking syrup and fold in the yogurt.
4 Beat the egg whites until they stand in soft peaks. Using a metal spoon, lightly stir 1 tablespoon of the beaten egg whites into the apricot purée mixture, then fold in the remainder.
5 Spoon the whip into stemmed glasses. Serve at once, or refrigerate until serving time. Serve with the wafers.

Cook's Notes

TIME
1¼ hours (including cooling time), but re-member that the apricots need to be soaked for a minimum of 4 hours before they are ready to be cooked.

DID YOU KNOW
Yogurt is a high-protein, low-calorie food, and dried apricots are a good source of iron. This dessert is suitable for anyone on a low-fat diet.

● 135 calories per portion

Mango yoghurt foam

SERVES 4

1 orange

2 large, ripe mangos, sliced (see Preparation)

1 teaspoon unflavored gelatin
3 tablespoons cold water
1¼ cups plain yogurt
2-3 tablespoons superfine sugar
1 egg white

1 Using a vegetable parer, pare several strips of rind from the orange. ⚠ With a small, sharp knife, shred the rind into matchstick sized strips.

2 Bring a small pan of water to a boil and blanch the strips for 2-3 minutes; drain and refresh under cold running water. Drain again, then pat dry on paper towels and set aside.

3 Squeeze the juice from the orange, then purée the prepared mangos and orange juice in a blender, or work the mangos through a strainer and stir in the orange juice.

4 Sprinkle the gelatin over the water in a small, heavy-bottomed pan. Leave to soak for 5 minutes, then set over very low heat for 1-2 minutes, until the gelatin is dissolved.

5 Stirring constantly with a wooden spoon, pour the dissolved gelatin in a thin stream onto the mango purée (see Cook's tip). Gradually beat in the yogurt, then sweeten to taste with superfine sugar.

6 In a spotlessly clean, dry bowl, beat the egg white until standing in stiff peaks. Using a large metal spoon, fold the egg white into the mango mixture. Taste and fold in more superfine sugar, if necessary.

7 Spoon the foam into 4 dessert dishes or stemmed glasses and decorate with the strips of orange rind. Serve within 2 hours.

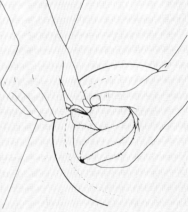

Melon mousse

SERVES 6

½ large honeydew melon, weighing about 1½ lb, seeded and pared
1 rounded tablespoon (1 envelope) unflavored gelatin
1 tablespoon lemon juice
1 tablespoon water
¼ cup superfine sugar
few drops of green food coloring
2 pinches ground ginger (optional)
2 egg whites
⅔ cup heavy cream

1 Sprinkle the gelatin over the lemon juice and water in a flameproof bowl and leave to soak for 5 minutes until spongy.

2 Meanwhile, cut the melon flesh into chunks and work through a strainer, [!] or purée in a blender then strain to remove fibers.

3 Pour the purée into a saucepan. Add the sugar and heat gently, stirring constantly, until the sugar is dissolved. Remove from the heat.

4 Stand the bowl containing the gelatin in a pan of gently simmering water and heat gently for 1-2 minutes until the gelatin has dissolved, stirring occasionally.

5 Stir the dissolved gelatin into the melon mixture, then add enough coloring to tint it a fairly strong green. Stir in ginger, if using. For a streaky effect, lightly stir in a little extra coloring.

6 Pour the mixture into a bowl; cool, then cover and refrigerate until beginning to set.

7 In a clean, dry bowl, beat the egg whites until standing in stiff peaks. Beat the cream in a separate bowl until it will just hold its shape. Fold the cream and then the egg whites into the melon mixture (see Preparation).

8 Divide the mixture between 6 individual glasses or glass bowls, cover and refrigerate for 8 hours, or overnight, until set. Serve chilled (see Serving ideas).

Tangerine jelly

SERVES 6

8 tangerines
2 tablespoons superfine sugar
2 tablespoons lemon juice
2 tablespoons water
1 rounded tablespoon unflavored
   gelatin
½ cup heavy cream
1 tablespoon orange liqueur
   (optional)

1 Rinse out 1-quart metal gelatin or ring mold with cold water and place it in the refrigerator to chill.

2 Squeeze the juice from 4 of the tangerines and strain into a measuring jug. Stir in the sugar, adding a little more to taste if liked.

3 Mix the lemon juice and water in a small bowl; sprinkle gelatin on top and leave to soak for about 5 minutes, until opaque and spongy. Then stand the bowl in a pan of hot water and stir until the gelatin is dissolved and the liquid is clear.

4 Remove the bowl from the pan and cool slightly. Pour the gelatin solution in a thin stream onto the strained fruit juice, stirring constantly. Make up to 2½ cups with water and refrigerate for about 1 hour, until just beginning to set.

5 Using a sharp serrated knife, pare the remaining tangerines, taking care to remove every bit of bitter white pith. Divide the fruit into segments and remove any pits.

6 Fold the segments through the almost set gelatin [!] and pour into the chilled mold. Refrigerate at least 4 hours, or overnight, until set.

7 Unmold the tangerine jelly carefully and allow to stand at room temperature for about 30 minutes to take the chill off the flavor. Lightly beat the cream and flavor with liqueur if liked. Use the cream to decorate the jelly or serve it in a separate bowl.

Cook's Notes

TIME
The jelly takes only 1 hour to prepare, but remember to allow at least 2 hours setting time.

WATCHPOINT
Wait until the gelatin is beginning to set before adding the fruit or it will sink to the bottom.

VARIATION
Use satsumas or mandarins if tangerines are not available.

● 150 calories per portion

Chocolate mousse special

SERVES 4

4 squares (4 oz) semi-sweet chocolate, broken into pieces
1 tablespoon water
few drops of vanilla
3 eggs, separated
20-24 sponge finger wafers (see Cook's tip)
chocolate curls and orange slices, to decorate (optional)

1 Put the chocolate, water and vanilla into a flameproof bowl. Set the bowl over a pan half full of simmering water and leave, stirring occasionally, until the chocolate is melted. Set aside to cool slightly.

2 In a large bowl, beat the egg yolks until pale. Add the melted chocolate and continue beating until the mixture is thick.

3 In a clean, dry bowl and using clean beaters, beat the egg whites until standing in stiff peaks. Fold the egg whites into the chocolate mixture with a large metal spoon.

4 Use half the wafers to line the base of an oblong 1-quart serving dish. (Trim the wafers, if necessary, so they fit neatly.)

5 Pour the chocolate mixture over the wafers, then cover with plastic wrap; refrigerate at least 2 hours.

6 To serve: Arrange the remaining wafers, cut in half, on top of the mousse. Decorate with chocolate flakes and orange slices, if liked, and serve chilled.

Cook's Notes

 TIME
This easy-to-make dessert takes only 30 minutes to prepare, but needs at least 2 hours chilling.

 COOK'S TIP
The number of sponge fingers you need depends on the shape of your serving dish.

 STORAGE
The mousse can be prepared up to the end of stage 5 and kept, covered, in the refrigerator for up to 48 hours.

SERVING IDEAS
Serve with a dish of sliced oranges.

● 275 calories per portion

Rich caramel mold

SERVES 6-8
⅓ cup sugar
3 tablespoons cold water
1¼ cups milk
2 × 6 inch sponge layers, cut in half
   horizontally
¼ cup apricot jam
1¼ cups light cream
4 large eggs, lightly beaten
vegetable oil, for greasing

TO FINISH
1¼ cups heavy cream
grated chocolate

1 Put the sugar and water into a small, heavy-bottomed saucepan and heat very gently, without stirring, until the sugar has dissolved. [!] Bring to a boil and boil rapidly until the syrup turns a rich caramel color. [!]
2 Immediately remove from heat and plunge base of pan into a bowl of cold water until the sizzling stops. Pour the milk onto the caramel, [!] then return to low heat and leave, stirring occasionally, until caramel has dissolved. Set aside.
3 Preheat the oven to 350°. Lightly oil a 1¼-quart charlotte mold or soufflé dish, line the base with waxed paper, then oil the paper.
4 Spread the cut side of each cake with jam. Arrange, jam-side-up, in the prepared mold. Lightly beat the cream, and then the caramel milk into the eggs; strain into the mold and leave for 15 minutes.
5 Lay a piece of oiled waxed paper over the top of the pudding. Stand the mold in a small roasting pan and pour in enough cold water to come halfway up the sides of the mold. Carefully transfer to the oven and bake for about 2 hours, until the custard is set.
6 Lift the mold out of the pan. Cool for 30 minutes, then remove waxed covering and run a palette knife around the side of the pudding. Invert a serving plate on top of the mold. Hold mold and plate firmly and invert them. Do not remove mold. Refrigerate for at least 3 hours, or overnight.
7 To serve: Lift off mold, remove paper, then mop up liquid on plate. with paper towels. Beat the heavy cream until standing in soft peaks, then pipe over pudding. Decorate with grated chocolate.

Cook's Notes

TIME
1 hour preparation (including decoration), 2 hours baking, plus chilling.

WATCHPOINTS
Make sure every granule of sugar has dissolved or the syrup will crystallize.
   Watch the caramel constantly as it can easily scorch.
   Stand well back as the milk will splutter for 1-2 seconds.

● 620 calories per portion

Ginger syllabub

SERVES 4

 5 tablespoons Advocaat
3 tablespoons ginger marmalade
   (see Cook's tip)
1¼ cups heavy cream
candied ginger or drained stem
   ginger, cut into small pieces, to
   decorate
crisp wafers, to serve

1 Mix the Advocaat and marmalade together in a small bowl.
2 Beat the cream until standing in soft peaks. ⚠️ Using a large metal spoon, fold the marmalade mixture into the cream.
3 Spoon the mixture into 4 stem-

Cook's Notes

TIME
10 minutes preparation, plus a minimum 30 minutes chilling time and a maximum of 2 hours.

COOK'S TIP
A jar of ginger marmalade is a useful pantry item, as it can be used to enliven both sweet and savory dishes. It makes a delicious filling for sponge cakes and 1 tablespoon is enough to pep up a beef casserole. Alternatively, try 1 tablespoon with cooked

rhubarb or in a rhubarb fool

WATCHPOINTS
Do not beat the cream until standing in stiff peaks, or the syllabubs will be too solid.
Syllabubs are always chilled before serving so that the flavors can mingle, but do not leave any longer than the specified time or the mixture will separate.

● 425 calories per portion

med dishes, cover with plastic wrap and refrigerate for at least 30 minutes, or up to 2 hours. ⚠️

4 Just before serving, decorate each syllabub with pieces of ginger. Serve chilled, with crisp wafers.

Cranberry brûlés

SERVES 4

½ lb cranberries (see Cook's tips)
5 tablespoons water
⅔ cup light brown sugar, or to taste
1½ teaspoons arrowroot

TOPPING
⅔ cup dairy sour cream (see Cook's tips)
2 tablespoons light brown sugar
large pinch of ground allspice

1 Put the cranberries and 4 table-spoons water into a heavy-bottomed saucepan. Cover and simmer gently for 5 minutes, then stir in ⅔ cup light brown sugar and cook for a further 3-4 minutes.
2 Blend the arrowroot with the remaining water and stir into the cranberry mixture. Bring to a boil and simmer for 1-2 minutes until thickened and no longer cloudy, stirring constantly.
3 Cool the cranberry mixture for 30 minutes, then taste and stir in more sugar if liked. Divide the mixture equally between 4 ramekins or other small flameproof dishes.
4 Preheat the broiler to high.
5 Spread the dairy sour cream over the cranberry mixture, almost to the edges. Mix the sugar and allspice and sprinkle evenly on top of the cream.
6 Place under the broiler for a few seconds, until the sugar is melted and bubbling. Remove immediately from the heat, leave to settle for 1-2 minutes, then serve hot. Alternatively, serve chilled (see Variation).

Marbled lime soufflé

SERVES 6
4 limes
1 rounded tablespoon (1 envelope)
    unflavored gelatin
6 tablespoons water
4 large eggs, separated
1 cup superfine sugar
1¼ cups heavy cream
few drops of green food coloring
unsalted pistachio nuts, blanched
    and chopped, to decorate (see
    Economy)

1 Prepare a 1¾-quart (6½-inch) ovenproof soufflé dish: Cut a 23 × 10 inch strip of aluminum foil or waxed paper. Fold in half lengthwise. Wrap the strip of aluminum foil around the dish so it stands above the rim and secure with masking tape. Lightly oil inside of collar, above rim of dish.
2 Finely grate the rind from 3 limes;

squeeze the juice from all the limes and measure out about ½ cup for the soufflé.
3 Sprinkle the gelatin over the water in a flameproof bowl. Leave to soak for 5 minutes until spongy, then set the bowl over a pan of simmering water and heat gently for 1-2 minutes until gelatin has dissolved, stirring occasionally. Remove gelatin liquid from heat and leave to cool slightly.
4 Meanwhile, put the egg yolks into a bowl with ¾ cup superfine sugar, the lime rind and reserved juice. Using an electric mixer, beat until very pale, thick and creamy.
5 Beat in the gelatin. Leave the mixture for 5-10 minutes, beating occasionally, until it is beginning to thicken.
6 In a clean, dry bowl, beat the egg whites until standing in stiff peaks. Beat in the remaining sugar, 1 tablespoon at a time, and continue beating until meringue is firm and glossy.
7 Meanwhile, beat the cream until standing in soft peaks.

8 Fold the whipped cream into the lime mixture, then gently fold in the meringue. Put half the mixture into another bowl and tint pale green with food coloring.
9 Put alternate spoonfuls of the 2 mixtures into prepared dish. Level the surface carefully, then chill for 4 hours, until set.
10 Remove tape from collar, then carefully peel away from soufflé with the aid of a round-bladed knife. Press chopped nuts around the sides of the soufflé. Serve as soon as possible.

Cook's Notes

TIME
40 minutes preparation, plus 4 hours chilling.

ECONOMY
Coarsely chopped toasted almonds would be a less expensive alternative.

● 465 calories per portion

Crêpe Alaska

SERVES 4
1 cup all-purpose flour
1½ teaspoons baking powder
¼ teaspoon salt
2 egg yolks
1 tablespoon superfine sugar
1 tablespoon vegetable oil
¾ cup milk
extra vegetable oil, for frying

FILLING
¾ cup apricot jam
1 tablespoon brandy or orange-
    flavored liqueur (see Economy)
1 can (about 1 lb) pineapple pieces,
    drained

MERINGUE
2 egg whites
½ cup superfine sugar
1 tablespoon flaked almonds

1 Preheat the oven to 425°.
2 Sift the flour, baking powder and salt into a bowl. Add the egg yolks, sugar, oil and milk and beat until just smoothly blended.
3 Brush a-6 inch heavy-bottomed skillet lightly with oil; place over moderately high heat. Remove from the heat and pour in about 2 tablespoons batter. Using the back of the spoon, spread the batter to the sides of the pan.
4 Return to the heat and cook until the bubbles burst on top. Loosen with a spatula, then turn the crêpe over and cook on the other side for a further 20-30 seconds, until browned. Lift onto waxed paper and keep warm.
5 Continue making crêpes, interleaving them with waxed paper, until you have about 7. Stir the batter frequently and grease the pan with more oil as necessary.
6 Warm the jam with the brandy in a small pan. Reserve 1 crêpe; spread the rest with warmed jam.
7 Place 1 crêpe, jam side up, on an ovenproof serving plate and top with a few pineapple pieces. Cover with another crêpe, jam side up. Continue layering in this way, ending with the reserved plain crêpe on top.
8 Make the meringue: In a clean, dry bowl, beat the egg whites until stiff, then beat in the sugar, 1 tablespoon at a time.
9 Swirl the meringue over the top and sides of crepe stack, taking it right down on to the plate. Sprinkle with the almonds. Bake immediately in the oven for 10 minutes, or until the meringue is tinged with brown and the nuts are golden. Serve at once, cut into wedges.

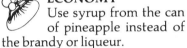

Cook's Notes

TIME
This spectacular dessert takes about 50 minutes to prepare (including 10 minutes baking time).

ECONOMY
Use syrup from the can of pineapple instead of the brandy or liqueur.

● 575 calories per portion

Raspberry soufflés

SERVES 4

1 cup raspberry purée
  (see Cook's tip)
1 tablespoon unflavored gelatin
3 tablespoons cold water
4 large eggs, separated
½ cup superfine sugar
1¼ cups heavy cream
vegetable oil, for greasing
crushed ratafias, extra superfine
  sugar and fresh hulled
  raspberries, to finish

1 Secure paper collars around 4 straight-sided, ¾-cup ramekins (see Preparation). Reserve 4 tablespoons of the purée.

2 Sprinkle the gelatin over the water in a cup; leave until spongy, then stand the cup in a bowl of very hot water until the gelatin is completely dissolved.

3 Meanwhile, beat the egg yolks and sugar together in a flameproof bowl over barely simmering water until thick and pale.

4 Remove from the heat. Beat in the dissolved gelatin and the remaining raspberry purée. Turn into a clean large bowl, cover and chill, stirring occasionally, until on the point of setting.

5 Beat 1 cup of the cream until it forms soft peaks. Using clean beaters, beat the egg whites until standing in soft peaks. Fold the cream and egg whites into the raspberry mixture. Divide between the prepared dishes, cover lightly and chill for about 2 hours, until set.

6 Remove the masking tape from paper collars; then gently peel away from the soufflés with the aid of a round-bladed knife. Press crushed ratafias around the sides.

7 Sweeten the reserve purée with superfine sugar, to taste. Spread 1 tablespoon purée over the top of each soufflé.

8 Beat the remaining cream with 2 teaspoons superfine sugar until standing in soft peaks. Decorate the top of each soufflé with raspberries, ratafias and piped cream.

Cook's Notes

TIME
50 minutes, plus chilling and setting.

COOK'S TIP
Work about 1-1¼ lb fresh or thawed frozen raspberries through a strainer or purée in a blender, then strain.

PREPARATION
The collars enable you to overfill the dish so that, when they are removed, the soufflés appear "risen."

Measure the depth and circumference of the dishes with string. Cut 4 strips of double thickness waxed paper, 1 inch longer and 1 inch deeper. Wrap 1 strip tightly around each dish and secure with masking tape. Lightly oil inside of paper, above rim.

● 505 calories per portion

Hot coffee soufflés

SERVES 4

3 tablespoons butter or margarine
¼ cup all-purpose flour
⅔ cup milk
3 eggs, separated
2 tablespoons superfine sugar
2 teaspoons coffee extract
melted butter, for greasing

SAUCE

¾ cup hot strong black coffee
1½-2 tablespoons sugar
1½ teaspoons arrowroot
1 tablespoon water
1-2 tablespoons Tia Maria

1 Preheat the oven to 350°. Brush the insides of four individual soufflé dishes with melted butter, then stand them on a cookie sheet.

2 Melt the butter in a fairly large saucepan, sprinkle in the flour and stir over low heat for 1-2 minutes until straw-colored. Remove from the heat and gradually stir in the milk. Return to the heat and simmer, stirring, until very thick and smooth. [!]

3 Remove from the heat, allow to cool for a few minutes, stir in the sugar and coffee extract. Then beat in the egg yolks one at a time.

4 In a clean, dry bowl, beat the egg whites until they stand in stiff peaks. Using a large metal spoon, lightly but thoroughly fold egg whites into the coffee mixture. [!]

5 Spoon into dishes. Mark a circle with a knife in the top of each soufflé. Bake in the oven, above center, for 25-30 minutes until risen well above the rims of the dishes and browned on top.

6 Meanwhile, make the sauce: Pour the hot coffee into a small pan and then stir in 1½ tablespoons sugar. Blend the arrowroot with the water, add to the sweetened coffee and simmer gently, stirring, until thickened and no longer cloudy. Remove from the heat and flavor with Tia Maria and more sugar, if liked. Keep hot. Serve the soufflés *immediately* after they are cooked, with a little of the sauce poured over them and the rest passed around separately in a serving jug.

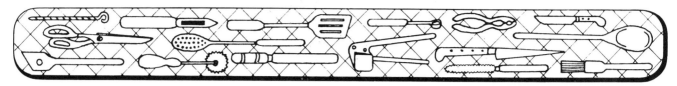

Baked mincemeat soufflé

SERVES 4-6

1 cup mincemeat
6 tablespoons dry wine
2 tablespoons brandy (optional)
¼ cup blanched almonds, chopped
4 large eggs, separated
pinch of salt
¼ teaspoon grated lemon or orange rind
2 tablespoons all-purpose flour
⅓ cup superfine sugar
confectioners' sugar, to dredge

1 Preheat the oven to 350°.
2 Put the mincemeat, wine, brandy (if using) and the blanched almonds into a saucepan and heat the mixture through gently.
3 Meanwhile, put the egg yolks, salt and lemon rind in a bowl and beat together lightly. Add the flour and continue beating until the mixture is pale and thick.
4 Beat the egg whites in a separate bowl until frothy. [!] Gradually beat in the superfine sugar and beat until the mixture forms soft peaks. Fold thoroughly into the egg yolk mixture with a metal spoon.
5 Pour the heated mincemeat mixture into a shallow ovenproof dish. Carefully spread the soufflé mixture on top.
6 Bake in the oven for about 15 minutes or until the topping is puffed up and golden brown.
7 Sift confectioners' sugar thickly over the top and serve at once.

Avocado ice cream

SERVES 6-8

2 ripe avocados
2 eggs
⅓ cup superfine sugar
1¼ cups light cream
finely grated rind and juice of
   1 large orange
1¼ cups heavy cream

1 Put the eggs and sugar into a bowl and beat together with a wooden spoon until thick and creamy.
2 Pour the light cream into a small saucepan and heat gently until almost boiling then immediately remove from the heat and pour onto the egg mixture, stirring vigorously. Leave the custard to cool.
3 Halve, pit and peel the avocados, then roughly chop the flesh. Purée with the orange rind and juice in a blender.
4 In a large bowl, beat the heavy cream until it forms soft peaks. Using a large metal spoon, fold in the avocado purée and the custard.
5 Turn into a large freezerproof container, cover and freeze until the mixture is frozen 1 inch around the edges. Scrape the mixture into a bowl and beat until smooth, then return to the container, cover and freeze until firm.
6 Transfer to the main part of the refrigerator about 30 minutes before serving to soften.

Cook's Notes

TIME
Preparation takes about 30 minutes, but you need to allow extra time for the custard to cool and about 6 hours freezing.

SERVING IDEAS
Scoop the ice cream into chilled glass dishes and serve with crisp wafers, to provide a texture contrast. Or, for a prettier effect, hollow out and scallop the edges of orange shells and then heap the ice cream into them.

●560 calories per portion

Mixed fruit ice

SERVES 4-6

1 can (about 6 oz) evaporated milk, chilled (see Watchpoint)

½ cup confectioners' sugar, sifted

2 bananas

juice of 2 lemons

1 can (13 oz) crushed pineapple

1 jar (about 6 oz) maraschino cherries, drained and halved with 2 tablespoons syrup reserved

1 Pour the milk into a large bowl and beat until thick and frothy, then beat in the confectioners' sugar.

2 Peel and mash the bananas with the lemon juice, then stir into the milk mixture together with the pineapple and its syrup.

3 Set aside a few cherries for decoration; stir the rest into the fruit and milk mixture together with the reserved syrup.

4 Pour the mixture into a rigid plastic container and freeze uncovered (see Cook's tip), for about 2 hours, until frozen around the edges. Loosen the frozen mixture with a fork and stir through the whole mixture. Cover and return to the freezer for a further 8 hours, or overnight, until firm.

5 To serve: Transfer the container to the main part of the refrigerator for about 30 minutes until softened, then scoop into dishes and decorate with reserved cherries.

Iced passion fruit dessert

SERVES 4

½ cup passion fruit pulp (see Preparation)
⅔ cup strawberry yogurt (see Variations)
1 teaspoon unflavored gelatin
½ cup water
3 tablespoons superfine sugar
2 egg whites

1 Put the passion fruit pulp into a large bowl with the yogurt and stir well until evenly blended.

2 Sprinkle the gelatin over the water in a flameproof bowl and leave to soak for 5 minutes, then stand bowl in a pan of gently simmering water for 1-2 minutes until the gelatin has completely dissolved, stirring occasionally.

3 Cool the gelatin slightly, then pour onto passion fruit mixture, stirring vigorously all the time to blend. Add the sugar and stir until dissolved.

4 Pour the mixture into a 1-quart metal or other freezerproof container. Leave, uncovered, in the freezer or freezing compartment of the refrigerator for 45-60 minutes until the mixture is frozen around the edges.

5 In an clean, dry bowl, beat egg whites until standing in stiff peaks. Turn passion fruit mixture into a large bowl and beat until smooth and creamy, then fold in egg whites with a large metal spoon.

6 Return mixture to the container, cover tightly and freeze for a further 4 hours or until firm. ✳

7 About 45 minutes before serving, transfer the mixture to the main part of the refrigerator to soften slightly. To serve: Carefully scoop into individual glasses.

Cook's Notes

TIME
15 minutes preparation, plus about 5 hours freezing and 45 minutes softening.

PREPARATION
You will need about 8 passion fruit. Cut in half, then scoop out the pulp.

SERVING IDEAS
This dessert is delicious served with slices of pineapple and sweet wafers.

VARIATIONS
Use passion fruit and melon or mandarin yogurt instead of strawberry. (In this case, the dessert will be pale yellow, rather than a pale apricot.)

✳ **FREEZING**
Seal the container, label and return to freezer for up to 6 weeks. To serve the passion fruit dessert: See stage 7.

● 95 calories per portion

Brown bread ice cream

SERVES 4

1 cup fresh whole wheat
  bread crumbs
2 tablespoons sugar
2 large eggs, separated
¼ cup light brown sugar (see
  Cook's tips)
⅔ cup heavy cream, whipped
  until in soft peaks
1 tablespoon coffee and chicory
  extract, or dark rum

1 Preheat the broiler to high. Mix the bread crumbs and sugar together; spread over the base of a small cookie sheet and toast under the broiler for about 5 minutes, turning occasionally, until golden and crunchy.
2 Turn the crunchy crumbs onto a plate and leave to cool completely, then crush coarsely with the back of a wooden spoon.
3 Beat the egg yolks with a fork until well blended, then set aside.
4 In a spotlessly clean and dry large bowl, beat egg whites until stiff. Beat in brown sugar, 1 tablespoon at a time. Using a large metal spoon, fold in the egg yolks, whipped cream, crushed bread crumbs and coffee and chicory.
5 Turn the mixture into a 1¼-quart metal container and cover securely with foil. Freeze (see Cook's tips) for 2 hours, stirring lightly every 30 minutes, ⚠ then leave for a further 2 hours, or until firm. ✳
6 Let the ice cream stand at room temperature for about 5 minutes, to soften slightly, before serving.

Cook's Notes

 TIME
5 minutes toasting plus cooling time for the bread crumbs, then 30-40 minutes preparation and about 4 hours freezing time.

COOK'S TIPS
Light brown sugar gives a lovely pale coffee color, but superfine sugar can be used for a whiter ice cream. Sift light brown sugar if it is lumpy.

To make the ice cream in the freezing compartment of the refrigerator: Turn the temperature to the lowest setting and chill the container 1 hour beforehand.

 SERVING IDEAS
Scoop into dessert bowls or stemmed glasses and top with fan wafers, or serve as an accompaniment to poached or canned fruit.

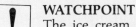 **FREEZING**
Overwrap, then return to the freezer and store for up to 3 months.

! **WATCHPOINT**
The ice cream mixture should be lightly stirred and turned over at regular times during the first 2 hours or the crumbs will sink.

● 320 calories per portion

Lime ice box pudding

SERVES 10

grated rind of 2 limes
juice of 3 limes
3 eggs, separated
½ cup superfine sugar
2 cups heavy cream
8 plain sweet wafers, crushed
fresh lime slices, to decorate

1 Line the base of an 8½ × 4½ × 2½ inches loaf pan with waxed paper.
2 Put the egg yolks in a large flameproof bowl over a pan half full of gently simmering water. Using a rotary or hand-held electric mixer, slowly beat in the sugar until pale and thick. [!] Remove from heat and stir in lime rind and juice.
3 Beat the cream until standing in soft peaks and fold into the lime mixture.

4 In a clean, dry bowl and using clean beaters, beat the egg whites until standing in soft peaks. Using a large metal spoon, fold the egg whites into the lime mixture.
5 Sprinkle a thin layer of wafer crumbs over the base of the pan. Carefully pour in the lime mixture and top with a layer of the remaining wafer crumbs.
6 Cover with foil, then place in the freezer compartment of the refrigerator or in the freezer and freeze for about 8 hours, or overnight, until firm. ✳
7 To serve (see Cook's tip): Uncover the pan, then run a palette knife around the edges of the pudding to loosen it. Turn out onto a flat serving plate and remove the waxed paper. Decorate the pudding with slices of lime and serve at once.

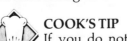

Cook's Notes

TIME
Preparation takes 40 minutes, plus about 8 hours freezing time.

COOK'S TIP
If you do not want to serve all the pudding at once, cut off as many slices as you need, then wrap the (undecorated) surplus in foil and return it to the freezer for up to 1 month.

WATCHPOINT
Make sure that the egg yolks and sugar are really thick before removing from the heat.

FREEZING
Freeze at the end of stage 6. Overwrap and return to the freezer for up to 1 month.

● 365 calories per portion

Cherries jubilee

SERVES 4

1 can (about 1 lb) pitted black cherries, drained, with syrup reserved
¼ cup brandy
2 teaspoons arrowroot
2 tablespoons water
large pinch of cinnamon
4 portions vanilla ice cream, to serve

1 Pour the brandy into a cup and stand in a pan or bowl of hot water to warm through gently.
2 In a small bowl, blend the arrow-root to a smooth paste with the water.
3 Pour the reserved cherry syrup into a saucepan. Add the cinnamon, then bring to a boil and boil briskly for 4 minutes, until reduced by one-quarter.
4 Remove pan from the heat ! and stir in the arrowroot mixture. Return to the heat, bring back to a boil and cook, stirring, until the mixture thickens and clears.
5 Add the cherries to the pan and simmer gently for 1-2 minutes.
6 Meanwhile, put the ice cream into 4 dessert bowls.
7 Turn off the heat under the pan. Pour the warmed brandy over the cherries and immediately set light to it. ! Let the flames die down completely, then spoon the cherries over the ice cream. Serve at once.

Tutti frutti ice cream

SERVES 4

⅔ cup heavy cream
2 cups vanilla pudding, cooled and beaten until smooth
¼ cup candied cherries, chopped
1 tablespoon cut mixed peel
2 tablespoons seedless or golden raisins
1 tablespoon chocolate morsels
¼ cup chopped mixed nuts (optional)
fan-shaped wafers, to serve

1 Beat the cream until just thickened, then stir in the pudding and mix until evenly combined. Turn the mixture into a shallow 1-quart freezerproof container. Freeze uncovered (see Cook's tips) for about 1 hour, or until frozen around the edges and slushy in the center.
2 Scrape the mixture into a bowl and beat well with a wooden spoon or hand-held electric mixer. Stir in the cherries, peel, raisins, chocolate and nuts, if using, making sure they are evenly distributed (see Economy). Return the mixture to the container, cover and freeze for a further 2 hours, or until solid.

3 Transfer the ice cream to the main part of the refrigerator for about 2 hours to soften slightly (see Cook's tips). Scoop into individual glass dishes and serve at once, with fan (or other shaped) wafers to give a texture contrast.

Cook's Notes

TIME
15 minutes preparation and about 3 hours freezing, plus softening time.

COOK'S TIPS
To shorten freezing time, refrigerate the pudding 2 hours in advance.
If using the freezing compartment of the refrigerator, turn it to its coldest setting 1 hour before making the ice cream. Return it to the original setting afterwards.
If you are in a hurry, soften the ice cream for 30 minutes at room temperature.

 FREEZING
The ice cream can be stored in the freezer for up to 2 months.

 FOR CHILDREN
Scoop the ice cream into cones and press half a chocolate flake into the top.

 ECONOMY
Beat 1 egg white until standing in soft peaks and fold into the mixture after adding the fruit and chocolate. This gives a greater volume.

● 405 calories per portion

Watermelon frappé

SERVES 4

1 watermelon (about 3 lb), seeded, pared and cut into cubes (see Cook's tips)
½ cup superfine sugar
finely grated rind and juice of 1 large orange
finely grated rind of ½ lemon
1 tablespoon lemon juice

1 Purée watermelon, in batches, in a blender, or crush to a pulp with a potato masher, then work the pulp through a strainer.

2 Put the sugar into a large bowl with the orange and lemon rind. Slowly stir in the orange and lemon juice. Add the watermelon purée, a little at a time, stirring constantly to dissolve the sugar.

3 Pour the mixture into a 1¼-quart rigid plastic container and freeze, uncovered, for about 3 hours, or until the mixture is slushy (see Cook's tips).

4 Turn the mixture into a large bowl and beat to break up large icy crystals. Return to the container, cover and freeze for a further 2-3 hours, until firm.

5 Transfer to the main part of the refrigerator and leave for 1-1½ hours, until softened. Mash the ice briefly with a fork to break up large lumps, then spoon into dishes and serve at once before it begins to melt (see Serving ideas).

Cook's Notes

 TIME
20 minutes preparation, plus freezing and softening time.

 DID YOU KNOW
Frappé means iced in French, and aptly describes this cooling dessert with its granular, icy texture.

 FREEZING
Overwrap the container, then return to the freezer for up to 2 months. To serve see stage 5.

● 160 calories per portion

 COOK'S TIPS
The easiest way to remove the seeds is to scrape them out with a fork.

If making the ice in the freezing compartment of the refrigerator, turn it to the lowest setting for 1 hour beforehand. Return to the original setting afterwards.

 SERVING IDEAS
This refreshing ice is an ideal dessert after a rich main course. Spoon it into stemmed glass dishes and provide long-handled spoons for easy eating.

Sicilian orange cassata

SERVES 6-8
⅔ cup orange juice
10 mini sponge cakes
¾ lb Ricotta cheese (see Buying
   guide)
½ cup superfine sugar
½ cup cut mixed peel
2 squares (2 oz) semi-sweet chocolate, broken up into small pieces
finely grated rind of 1 orange
3 teaspoons medium sherry
vegetable oil, for greasing

TO DECORATE
⅔ cup heavy cream
3 orange slices, halved

1 Brush a 1¼-quart bombe mold or
pudding basin very lightly with oil.
Pour the orange juice into a shallow
bowl.
2 Using three-quarters of the trifle
sponge cakes, dip one side of each
into the orange juice and use to line
completely the sides and base of
the mold with the darker sugar-
coated sides facing inwards (see
Preparation).
3 Place all the Ricotta cheese in a
large bowl and stir in the remaining
ingredients, mixing well. Spoon
into the prepared mold and level the
surface. If necessary, trim the ends
of the sponge cakes level with the
top of the filling.
4 Dip the remaining sponge cakes
in the orange juice and use to cover
the top of the cassata. Cover and
refrigerate overnight.
5 Uncover, then carefully run a
palette knife down the sides of the
sponge lining to loosen. Invert a
serving plate on top of the mold.
Hold the plate and mold firmly and
invert, giving a sharp shake halfway
around. Carefully remove the mold
from the cassata.
6 To decorate: Beat the cream until
standing in stiff peaks, then spoon
into a pastry bag fitted with a star
nozzle. Pipe cream decoratively
around base of the cassata, then
pipe a ring on top. Arrange the
halved orange slices overlapping on
top of the ring of cream and serve at
once or refrigerate for up to 1 hour
before serving.

Cook's Notes

 TIME
30-40 minutes to make
cassata, plus chilling
overnight and 10 minutes for
decorating.

PREPARATION
To line the mold with
trifle sponge cakes:

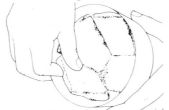

*Press a soaked sponge cake into
center of base, then press the rest
against the sides.*

 DID YOU KNOW
This is a version of the
famous Sicilian sponge
cake that is traditionally served
at weddings to celebrate the
start of a new life.

BUYING GUIDE
Ricotta is made from
the whey of cow's milk
and is a smooth, mild cheese. It
is always sold fresh and is available from Italian delicatessens
or the delicatessen counters of
some large supermarkets. If it is
unavailable, use curd or cottage
cheese instead but pass through
a strainer before using.

● 520 calories per portion

Grapefruit ice

SERVES 4

 grated rind and juice of 2 grapefruit
½ cup superfine sugar
 1¼ cups water
2 grapefruit slices, quartered, to
   decorate

1 Place the sugar and water in a saucepan and heat gently until the sugar has dissolved, then bring to a boil and boil for about 5 minutes, without stirring, until a thick syrup is formed.
2 Remove the syrup from the heat and leave until completely cold. [!]
3 Add the grapefruit rind and juice to the cold syrup and pour into a 1¼-quart shallow freezerproof pan or ice cube tray without the divisions. Freeze in the freezer compartment of a refrigerator or in the freezer for about 30 minutes (see Cook's tip) until slushy.
4 Remove from the freezer and stir well with a metal spoon until evenly blended.
5 Return to the freezer for 30 minutes, then stir again. Repeat this process once more, then cover and freeze for at least 8 hours.
6 To serve: Stir the mixture well, to break up any large pieces of ice, then spoon into glasses or small dishes. Decorate each portion with quartered grapefruit slices. Serve at once (see Serving ideas).

Pear wine sherbet

SERVES 4

**4 firm dessert pears, pared, cored
    and sliced (see Buying guide)**
**⅔ cup white wine (see Buying
    guide)**
⅓ cup superfine sugar
strip of lemon rind
maraschino cherries, to decorate

1 Put wine, sugar and rind in a saucepan and stir over low heat until the sugar has dissolved. Bring to a boil, add the pears, then cover the pan and poach the pears gently for about 5 minutes, or until opaque. Remove the pan from the heat and set aside to cool.

2 Discard the lemon rind, reserve a few pear slices for decoration, then purée the cold mixture in a blender or press it through a strainer.

3 Pour into a freezer container, cover and freeze for several hours until firm (see Cook's tips).

4 Remove from the freezer and turn into a large bowl. ⚠️ Break the sherbet up with a fork, then beat it well until slushy.

5 Spoon the mixture back into its freezer container, cover and return to the freezer for a further 3-4 hours until firm.

6 Remove the sherbet from the freezer and allow it to soften at room temperature for about 15 minutes. Then spoon it into individual glasses and serve decorated with pear slices and maraschino cherries.

Cook's Notes

TIME
Preparation takes only about 20 minutes, but remember to allow several hours for freezing time.

FREEZING
The sherbet can be stored in the freezer for up to 2 months.

BUYING GUIDE
Choose firm pears such as Conference or Comice for this sherbet. Avoid Williams which will be too soft.

It is worth choosing a good wine, or the flavor of the finished sherbet will be disappointing. Choose sweet or dry according to your taste.

WATCHPOINT
If the sherbet is too firm to mash, let it soften slightly at room temperature.

COOK'S TIPS
To make the sherbet in the freezing compartment of an ordinary refrigerator, use a pre-chilled shallow metal tray for freezing the sherbet and turn the refrigerator down to its coldest setting at least 1 hour before you start making the sherbet. This will help speed up the freezing process.

VARIATION
Decorate the sherbet with a few sprigs of fresh mint in season.

● 140 calories per portion

Mint sherbet

SERVES 4

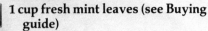

- 1 cup fresh mint leaves (see Buying guide)
- 2 cups water
- ½ cup superfine sugar
- thinly pared rind and juice of 2 lemons
- few drops of green food coloring
- 1 egg white
- sprigs of mint, to decorate

1 Pour the water into a heavy-bottomed saucepan. Add the sugar and lemon rind and stir over low heat until the sugar has dissolved, then bring to a boil and simmer, without stirring, for 5 minutes.

2 Remove the syrup from the heat, stir in the lemon juice and mint leaves and leave to cool completely.

3 Strain the syrup into a 1-quart freezerproof container. Stir in the coloring, then cover and freeze (see Cook's tips) for about 3 hours, or until the mixture is frozen about ½ inch around the edges and slushy in the center.

4 Turn the mint mixture into a large bowl and mash well with a fork (see Cook's tips). In a clean, dry bowl, beat the egg white until standing in stiff peaks. Beat the mint mixture to break up large lumps, then beat in the egg white about a third at a time and continue beating until evenly incorporated.

5 Return the mixture to the container, cover ✳ and freeze for a further 3 hours, or until firm.

6 To serve: Allow the sherbet to soften for 5 minutes at room temperature, then scoop into stemmed glasses. Decorate with a sprig of mint and serve at once.

Cook's Notes

TIME
20 minutes preparation (excluding cooling the syrup), plus 6 hours freezing.

FREEZING
Overwrap container, seal, label and return to freezer for up to 3 months.

COOK'S TIPS
If using freezing compartment of refrigerator, turn to coldest setting at least 1 hour before making the sherbet. Remember to return it to original setting afterwards.

If the mint mixture is solid, allow it to soften slightly before mashing it with the fork.

BUYING GUIDE
Any variety of mint — spearmint, peppermint or applemint — is excellent for this sherbet. As they will grow profusely it is worth asking friends with gardens if they have any mint to spare. Do not use dried mint for this recipe; it will not give a good flavor.

● 105 calories per portion

Tea sherbet

SERVES 8

10½ teaspoons China tea (see Buying guide)
⅔ cup superfine sugar
2½ cups boiling water
juice of 2 lemons
4 egg whites

1 Put the tea into a large flameproof bowl with the sugar. Pour over the boiling water and stir until the sugar has dissolved, then cover and leave to stand for 1 hour.

2 Strain the tea through a very fine strainer into a jug. Stir in the lemon juice, then pour into a 1¼-quart metal loaf pan or other freezerproof container. Cover tightly with foil and freeze in the freezer (or freezing compartment of refrigerator turned to its coldest setting) for 2½ hours, or until half-frozen and slushy.

3 Remove from the freezer, turn into a bowl and mash with a fork to break up the ice crystals, then beat briefly until smooth. Return to container, cover and freeze for a further 2 hours, or until firm.

4 In a clean, dry bowl, beat egg whites until standing in soft peaks.

5 Remove the tea ice from freezer, turn into a large bowl and break up with a fork as before, mashing well. Beat the ice until smooth, then slowly beat in the egg whites. Return the mixture to the container, cover and freeze for a further 4 hours, until firm. ✳

6 To serve: Remove from the freezer and soften at room temperature for 20-30 minutes. Scoop or spoon into small serving dishes. Serve at once (see Serving ideas).

Cook's Notes

 TIME
10-15 minutes preparation, plus 1 hour standing and about 8½ hours freezing, plus softening time.

 BUYING GUIDE
Choose black China tea: Either Lapsang Suchong or Keemam, both of which are available from good supermarkets and specialist food stores. Do not use Indian or other teas, they are too strong.

 FREEZING
Seal the container, label and return to the freezer for up to 3 months. Soften and serve as in stage 6.

SERVING IDEAS
The subtle, slightly bitter, flavor of this sherbet is best complemented with a sweet fruit such as strawberries or raspberries. Candied fruit or rose petals would make a pretty decoration.

● 80 calories per portion

Lemon layer sponge

SERVES 4

3 large eggs, separated
3 tablespoons all-purpose flour
3 tablespoons superfine sugar
¾ cup milk
2 tablespoons butter, melted
grated rind and juice of 1 lemon
confectioners' sugar, to dredge
light cream, to serve

1 Preheat the oven to 325°.
2 Place the egg yolks, flour, super-fine sugar, milk, butter, lemon juice and rind in a large bowl and beat until smoothly blended.
3 In a clean dry bowl, and using clean beaters, beat the egg whites until stiff. Gently but thoroughly fold them into the lemon mixture, using a large metal spoon.
4 Spoon the mixture into a buttered 1¼-quart baking dish standing in a roasting pan. Pour enough hot water into the pan to come about 1 inch up the side of the dish (see Preparation).
5 Bake the sponge in the oven for about 1 hour until risen, golden, and just firm to the touch. Remove the dish from the pan. Sift confectioners' sugar thickly over the top of the sponge. Serve warm, with cream.

Cook's Notes

TIME
About 15 minutes to prepare and 1 hour to bake.

PREPARATION
Standing the dish in a pan of hot water for baking helps keep the sponge deliciously soft and moist.

During baking, the mixture separates into layers: A light sponge on top and a rich custard sauce underneath.

● 210 calories per portion

Creamy blackcurrant cheesecake

MAKES 8-10 SLICES

7 tablespoons butter
¼ cup superfine sugar
½ lb shortbread cookies, finely crushed
butter, for greasing

FILLING AND TOPPING

1 lb cream cheese (see Buying guide)
¾ cup superfine sugar
3 eggs, separated
finely grated rind of ½ lemon
few drops of vanilla
⅔ cup heavy cream
5 teaspoons unflavored gelatin
5 tablespoons water
1 can (about 14 oz) blackcurrant pie filling
lemon twists (optional)

1 Grease a deep, 9-inch round cake pan with a loose base.

2 Put the butter and sugar into a small, heavy-bottomed saucepan and stir over low heat until melted. Remove from the heat and stir in the cookie crumbs, then press the mixture evenly over the base of the prepared pan. Refrigerate.

3 Put the cheese into a large bowl and beat until softened. Beat in ⅓ cup sugar, the egg yolks, lemon rind, vanilla and cream.

4 Sprinkle the gelatin over the water in a flameproof bowl. Leave to soak for 5 minutes until spongy, then stand the bowl in a pan of barely simmering water for 1-2 minutes, stirring occasionally, until the gelatin has dissolved.

5 Allow the gelatin to cool slightly, then beat it into the cheese mixture. Leave in a cool place for about 15 minutes, until on point of setting.

6 In a clean, dry bowl, beat the egg whites until standing in stiff peaks, then gradually beat in the remaining sugar. Fold the meringue into the cheese mixture.

7 Turn filling into prepared pan and level the surface. Cover and chill for at least 3 hours, until set.

8 To serve: Loosen cake with a palette knife, then remove sides of pan. Spread pie filling over the top. Add lemon twists, if liked.

Cook's Notes

TIME
1 hour preparation, plus 3 hours setting and about 5 minutes for finishing.

BUYING GUIDE
Philadelphia (or an equivalent supermarket brand) gives best results and won't turn grainy.

● 665 calories per slice

Date and walnut baked apples

SERVES 4

4 large cooking apples (see
  Buying guide)
6 tablespoons natural unsweetened
  apple juice
whipped heavy cream, to serve

FILLING
⅓ cup dates, pitted and coarsely
  chopped
2 tablespoons shelled walnuts,
  chopped
2 tablespoons dark brown sugar
½ teaspoon cinnamon

1 Preheat the oven to 350°.
2 Using an apple corer or a small sharp knife, remove the core from each apple. Score the skin around the middle of each apple with a sharp knife (see Cook's tip).
3 Make the filling: Mix together the dates, walnuts, sugar and cinnamon in a bowl. Use to fill cavities, pressing down firmly with the back of a teaspoon.
4 Place in an ovenproof dish, then pour apple juice around apples.
5 Bake in oven for 50-60 minutes, basting occasionally with the apple juice, until the apples are soft when pierced through the center with a sharp knife.
6 Serve at once, accompanied by whipped heavy cream.

Cook's Notes

TIME
15 minutes preparation;
50-60 minutes cooking.

VARIATION
Replace the dates with chopped figs.

COOK'S TIP
Scoring the apples will prevent the skins from exploding during baking.

BUYING GUIDE
Choose Winesap apples, each weighing about ½ lb.

● 175 calories per portion

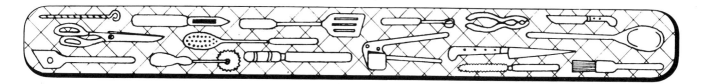

Magic chocolate pudding

SERVES 4
¾ cup all-purpose flour
1 teaspoon baking powder
2 tablespoons cocoa powder
pinch of salt
1 cup butter or margarine,
    softened
½ cup superfine sugar
½ teaspoon vanilla
2 eggs, lightly beaten
1-2 tablespoons milk
butter, for greasing

SAUCE
½ cup light brown sugar
2 tablespoons cocoa powder
1¼ cups boiling water

1 Preheat the oven to 375°. Lightly grease a 1¾-quart fairly deep ovenproof pie dish.
2 Sift flour and baking powder into a bowl with cocoa powder and salt, then set aside.
3 Beat the butter and superfine sugar together until pale and fluffy, then beat in the vanilla. Beat in the eggs, a little at a time, adding 1 tablespoon of the flour mixture with the last few additions of egg. Gradually stir in the remaining flour mixture and mix well, then add enough milk to give a smooth dropping consistency.
4 Spoon the mixture into the prepared dish, spread it evenly.
5 Make the sauce: Mix together the brown sugar and cocoa powder, then gradually blend in the water, stirring vigorously to avoid lumps. Pour the sauce over the mixture in the pie dish (see Cook's tip).
6 Bake the pudding in the oven for about 35-40 minutes, or until the pudding is well risen and browned and the chocolate sauce beneath is syrupy. Serve while hot. (See Serving ideas).

Cook's Notes

 TIME
15 minutes preparation and 40 minutes baking.

 COOK'S TIP
This quick and easy pudding, which is very popular with children, has the added bonus of an "instant" chocolate sauce that cooks with the mixture in the oven. Do not worry if the mixture looks unpromising when you pour over the sauce: During baking it rises above the sauce.

 SERVING IDEAS
The pudding is rich enough to eat as it is, but if you are feeling really indulgent, serve it with ice cream or whipped cream.

 SPECIAL OCCASION
Use dark rum instead of milk. Stir in ¼ cup chopped walnuts or blanched almonds at the end of stage 3.

● 520 calories per portion

Queen of puddings

SERVES 4
1 cup fresh white bread crumbs
2 tablespoons sugar
grated rind of ½ lemon
2 cups milk
1 tablespoon butter or margarine
2 egg yolks
5 tablespoons lemon curd
butter or margarine, for greasing

MERINGUE
2 egg whites
⅓ cup superfine sugar

1 Mix the bread crumbs, sugar and lemon rind together in a bowl. In a small saucepan, bring the milk and butter almost to a boil, then remove from the heat and pour over the crumb mixture. Stir well, then leave to soak for 10-15 minutes.

2 Meanwhile, preheat the oven to 350°. Grease a 1-quart ovenproof pie dish.

3 Beat the egg yolks into the milky crumbs, then spoon the mixture into the dish and spread it evenly. Bake in the oven for 35-40 minutes, until just set in the center. ⚠

4 Remove the dish from the oven and spread the lemon curd over the pudding. In a spotlessly clean and dry bowl, beat the egg whites until standing in stiff peaks. Reserve 2-3 teaspoons of the superfine sugar; beat the remaining sugar into the egg whites, 1 tablespoon at a time, and continue beating until the meringue is stiff and glossy. Spread it over the pudding, then form into peaks (see Preparation) and sprinkle over the reserved sugar.

5 Return the dish to the oven and bake for 10-15 minutes, until the surface of the meringue is crisp and lightly browned.

6 Serve the pudding at once, straight from the dish.

Cook's Notes

TIME
Preparation and cooking take about 1¼ hours.

⚠ WATCHPOINT
The pudding should be only just firm when the lemon curd is spread over it because the dish is returned to the oven to set the meringue.

VARIATION
Omit the lemon rind and add ¼ cup desiccated coconut to the bread crumbs and sugar. Replace the lemon curd with red jam.

❓ DID YOU KNOW
Queen of puddings is a traditional English pudding, dating back to the 19th century. The original recipe used red jam rather than lemon curd.

PREPARATION
How to cover the pudding with meringue:

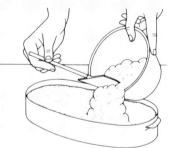

1 Pile the meringue on top of the pudding and spread it evenly, covering the surface completely.

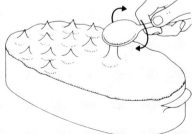

2 Using a light circular action, peak the meringue decoratively with the back of a metal spoon.

● 330 calories per portion

Tropical crumble

SERVES 4-6

4 oranges, pared and chopped
4 fresh apricots, pitted and
    chopped or 8 canned apricot
    halves, chopped
2 large bananas, peeled and sliced
¼ lb fresh pineapple,
    chopped, or canned pineapple
    chunks
light cream or ice cream, to serve

TOPPING
½ cup all-purpose flour
½ teaspoon ground ginger
⅓ cup rolled oats
¼ cup desiccated coconut
⅔ cup dark brown sugar
5 tablespoons butter, melted.

1 Preheat the oven to 350°.
2 First make the topping: Sift the flour and ginger into a mixing bowl. Add the oats, coconut and sugar and mix together. Stir in the melted butter.
3 Put all the fruit into a deep oven-proof dish, turning the banana slices in the juice from the oranges to prevent them from discoloring.
4 Sprinkle the topping evenly over the fruit and press down gently to level the surface.
5 Bake for about 40 minutes or until the fruit mixture is bubbling up around the edge of the topping. Serve hot with light cream or, if preferred, ice cream.

Cook's Notes

TIME
The preparation of the fruit and the crumble topping will take about 20 minutes. The cooking time is about 40 minutes.

COOK'S TIP
If using canned pineapple, try to find a can that has unsweetened syrup,

because the topping mixture for the crumble is itself very sweet.

VARIATIONS
Use other fruits such as apple or rhubarb with the same crumble topping. If you use dried fruit allow an extra 3 hours soaking time.

● 510 calories per portion

Bread and butter pudding

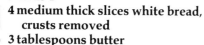

SERVES 4

- 4 medium thick slices white bread, crusts removed
- 3 tablespoons butter
- ⅓ cup golden raisins
- 2 tablespoons superfine sugar
- 2 large eggs
- 1¼ cups milk
- ¼ teaspoon ground nutmeg

1 Butter the bread well on one side. Cut each slice into 4.

2 Layer bread, buttered side up, in a well-greased 1¼-quart ovenproof dish, sprinkling raisins and sugar between each layer and on top of the last layer.

3 Beat the eggs and milk together and strain over the bread. Leave to stand in a cool place for 30 minutes.

4 Preheat the oven to 350°.

5 Sprinkle the nutmeg over the pudding and bake in the oven for 25-30 minutes until set and golden brown. Serve hot.

Cook's Notes

TIME
Preparation 10 minutes, cooking time 30 minutes, but allow another 30 minutes soaking time.

ECONOMY
This is an excellent way of using up stale white or whole wheat bread.

● 665 calories per portion

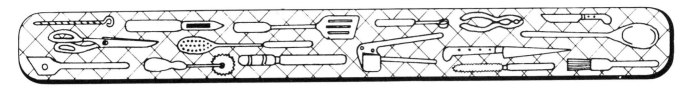

Sherry trifle

SERVES 4-6

2 sponge layers, cut in half
   horizontally
⅓ cup raspberry jam
¼ cup medium sherry
1 can (about 14 oz) raspberries,
   drained with syrup reserved
3 large eggs
2 tablespoons superfine sugar
2½ cups milk
1 teaspoon vanilla
1¼ cups heavy whipping
   cream
candied cherries, halved
a little angelica, to finish

1 Spread the sponges with the jam, then sandwich together again. Cut into 1 inch pieces and arrange in the base of a glass serving bowl.
2 Stir the sherry into the reserved raspberry syrup, then pour over the sponges. Scatter the raspberries over the top.

3 Beat the eggs and sugar lightly together in a large bowl (see Cook's tip). Heat the milk until almost boiling in a small saucepan, then pour onto the egg and sugar mixture, beating constantly.
4 Strain the mixture into a heavy-bottomed pan. [!] Cook over low heat for 10-15 minutes, [!] stirring constantly with a wooden spoon, until the custard is thick enough to coat the back of the spoon. Remove from the heat, stir in the vanilla and leave to cool for 10 minutes.
5 Pour the custard over the raspberries and sponges and leave to cool completely. Cover and refrigerate for 3-4 hours, or overnight.
6 Beat the cream until it forms soft peaks. Spread one-third of the cream over the custard and mark the surface with a fork or small spatula, if liked. Put the remaining cream into a pastry bag fitted with a large star nozzle. Pipe a border of cream and a lattice on the trifle, then decorate with cherries and angelica. Serve at once, or cover and refrigerate for 2-3 hours.

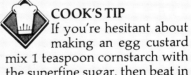

Nutty apple crumble

SERVES 4

3 large dessert apples (total weight about 1 lb)

⅓ cup golden raisins
¼ cup light brown sugar
2 tablespoons water

CRUMBLE TOPPING
1 cup whole wheat flour
1 teaspoon ground allspice
½ cup chilled butter or margarine, cubed
½ cup walnuts, roughly chopped
¼-⅓ cup light brown sugar, according to taste

1 Preheat the oven to 375°.
2 Make the crumble topping: Put the flour in a mixing bowl with the allspice. Stir well to mix. Add the butter and cut it in with a round-bladed knife, then cut in the pieces until the mixture resembles coarse bread crumbs. Stir in the walnuts and sugar to taste, then set aside.
3 Pare, core and slice the apples (see Cook's tip) and layer them with the raisins and the sugar in a well-buttered 1¾-quart ovenproof dish. Sprinkle over the water.
4 Sprinkle the crumble mixture over the apples and press down lightly to level the surface.
5 Bake in the oven for 40-50 minutes or until the crumble topping is crisp and golden and the apples are tender. Serve hot or warm.

Cook's Notes

TIME
Preparation 15 minutes, cooking time 50 minutes.

SERVING IDEAS
This sweet dessert is best served with a sharp-tasting plain yogurt, rather than custard or cream.

WATCHPOINT
Make sure the butter is well chilled or it will be impossible to rub in. Do not overwork the mixture or it will become sticky and doughy and impossible to work with.

COOK'S TIP
Slice the apples thinly so they will be cooked at the same time as the topping.

VARIATION
Use green apples and the full amount of sugar for the topping.

● 560 calories per portion

Jam soufflé omelets

MAKES 2, TO SERVE 4

6 eggs
2 tablespoons superfine sugar
few drops of vanilla
3 tablespoons butter
6-8 tablespoons jam, warmed
¼ cup confectioners' sugar, to dredge

1 Make the first omelet: Separate 3 of the eggs, placing the whites in a clean, dry bowl. Beat the egg whites until standing in soft peaks. In a separate bowl, beat the egg yolks with half the sugar and 1-2 drops vanilla.

2 Preheat the broiler to high.

3 Melt half the butter in an omelet pan or skillet with a base diameter of 8 inches. Meanwhile, quickly fold the beaten egg yolks into the egg whites with a large metal spoon.

4 As soon as the butter is foaming, pour in the egg mixture and turn down the heat to low. Cook the omelet, without stirring, for

Cook's Notes

TIME
Each omelet takes about 10 minutes to prepare and cook.

WATCHPOINTS
The size of the pan is important: If it is too small the omelet will be too thick to fold; if it is too large the omelet will be disappointingly thin.
If stirred, the omelet will lose its light, fluffy texture.

COOK'S TIP
If you only need to serve 2 people, make just 1 omelet, but if serving 4, do not try to keep the first omelet hot while cooking the second one. Pick an occasion when it does not matter if everyone is served at one time. To cut down the time between servings beat the second batch of egg whites while the first omelet is cooking.

DID YOU KNOW
This type of sweet omelet is traditionally decorated with a criss-cross pattern, made by placing heated metal skewers on top of the folded omelet until the confectioners' sugar is caramelized, as shown in the photograph.

● 340 calories per portion

2-3 minutes, until the underside is set and golden. Then place the pan under the broiler for 2-3 minutes, until the top of the omelet is golden brown.

5 Spread half the warmed jam over one-half of the omelet. Using a large palette knife or spatula, fold the omelet in half to enclose jam.

6 Slide the omelet onto a warmed dish and sift half the confectioners' sugar over the top. Cut across in half and serve at once.

7 Use the remaining ingredients to made the second omelet in the same way (see Cook's tip).

Orange castles

SERVES 4

1 package (about ¼ lb) orange
    flavored gelatin
1 cup boiling water
¾ cup cold water
8 oz cream cheese

TO DECORATE
about ½ cup desiccated
    coconut
1 can (about 11 oz) mandarin orange
    segments, drained
"leaves" of angelica

1 Put the gelatin in a jug, add 1 cup boiling water and stir until dissolved. Then gradually mix in the ¾ cup cold water.

2 Refrigerate the gelatin until beginning to set around the edges. Beat the cream cheese until smooth then gradually beat in the setting gelatin.

3 Rinse out four ⅔ cup molds with water (see Cook's tips). Divide the gelatin mixture between the prepared molds, cover with plastic wrap and refrigerate for 1-2 hours, until set.

4 Unmold the gelatins, one at a time: Run a round-bladed knife around the sides of the gelatin to loosen it. Dip the base of the mold in a bowl of hot water for 2-3 seconds, then invert a dampened dessert plate on top. Hold the mold and plate firmly and invert them, giving a sharp shake halfway around (see Cook's tips). Lift off the mold.

5 Sprinkle the coconut over the gelatins, covering the tops and as much of the sides as possible. Using the tip of a round-bladed knife, lift the loose coconut from the plates and gently press it onto the sides of the gelatins.

6 Arrange mandarin orange segments on the top and around the base of each gelatin, then decorate with "leaves" of angelica. Serve at once, or refrigerate for up to 2 hours.

Cook's Notes

TIME
30 minutes preparation (including decorating), plus setting time.

COOK'S TIPS
You can reduce setting time by chilling the dessert for 1 hour beforehand.

Empty plastic yogurt, cream or salad cartons make ideal molds for this dessert if you do not have individual castle gelatin or dariole molds.

The gelatins can be difficult to turn out; you may need to repeat dipping and shaking.

SPECIAL OCCASION
Turn gelatins out onto glass dishes. Sprinkle mandarins around base of gelatins with orange liqueur.

● 235 calories per gelatin

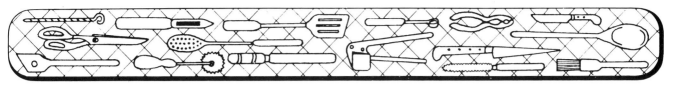

Iced chocolate boxes

MAKES 6

1 pint block chocolate ice cream (see Watchpoint)
24 peppermint chocolates (see Buying guide)
⅔ cup heavy cream
1 can (about ¾ lb) mandarin orange segments, drained
6 small sprigs fresh mint, to decorate (optional)

1 Cut the ice cream into 6 equal cubes and place on a freezerproof plate. Press 1 chocolate onto 4 sides of each cube leaving the top and bottom plain. Return to the freezer, or freezing compartment of the refrigerator ✳ while you prepare the cream.

2 Beat the cream until thick, but not stiff, then put into a pastry bag fitted with a large star nozzle (see Cook's tip).
3 Remove the chocolate boxes from the freezer and pipe the cream on the top of each box. Top with mandarin orange segments and a sprig of mint, if liked. Place on chilled, individual serving plates and serve immediately, before the ice cream melts.

Cook's Notes

 TIME
Preparation takes only 15 minutes.

 WATCHPOINT
Be sure to buy block ice cream; the soft-scoop variety is not suitable.

 BUYING GUIDE
Wafer-thin plain chocolates with peppermint fondant cream centers are best; they are sold in ½ lb boxes, each containing about 26.

 COOKS' TIP
Instead of piping the cream, you can pile it on top of each box with a spoon.

 FREEZING
Prepare the boxes up to the end of stage 1; open freeze, then place in a single layer in a rigid container. Cover and return to the freezer for up to 1 month. Use straight from the freezer; decorate and serve.

● 300 calories per portion

Raisin semolina

SERVES 4-6

2½ cups milk
¼ cup semolina
¼ cup seedless raisins
1 egg, beaten
¼ cup soft brown sugar
½ teaspoon cinnamon
1 tablespoon butter or margarine,
**   shaved into flakes**
melted butter or margarine,
**   for greasing**

1 Brush the inside of a 2½-cup flameproof dish with butter.
2 Pour the milk into a heavy-bottomed saucepan and heat gently until just below boiling point. Sprinkle in the semolina and stir until the mixture comes to a boil. Add the raisins, then reduce the heat and cook gently for 15 minutes, stirring frequently.
3 Preheat the broiler to high.
4 Remove the pan from the heat.

Allow the semolina mixture to cool slightly, then beat in the egg, a little at a time. ⚠ Return the pan to low heat and cook, stirring, for 1 minute.
5 Turn the semolina mixture into the prepared dish and level the surface. Mix the sugar with the

cinnamon and sprinkle over the surface of the semolina, then dot with the butter.
6 Place under the broiler for 2-3 minutes, until the sugar is melted and bubbling. ⚠ Serve hot or cold, straight from the dish.

Cook's Notes

⏰ **TIME**
Preparation and cooking take about 25 minutes.

⚠ **WATCHPOINTS**
Beat the egg into the mixture quickly, otherwise it will start to set.
Watch the topping constantly; once the sugar starts to color it darkens very rapidly.

🥣 **SERVING IDEAS**
Divide the cooked semolina between 4-6 ramekin dishes. Add the sugar topping and butter and caramelize. Just before serving, top with whipped cream.

❓ **DID YOU KNOW**
Semolina is made from the grains of durum wheat. It is a handy pantry item for savory as well as sweet dishes but, once opened, it goes stale very quickly and should be used within 3 months.

👨‍🍳 **COOK'S TIP**
If more convenient, you can finish the semolina in the oven, preheated to 375°. It will take about 10 minutes for the sugar to caramelize.

● 255 calories per portion

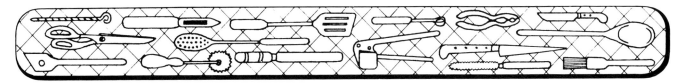

Treacle tart

SERVES 4-6

1 package (about 9 oz) pie crust
   sticks, prepared
1 cup dark corn syrup (see Cook's
   tips)
1½ cups white bread crumbs, made
   from stale bread
grated rind and juice of ½ lemon
heavy cream or custard, to serve
   (optional)

1 Preheat the oven to 400°.
2 Roll out the pastry thinly on a
lightly floured surface and use to
line an 8-inch loose-bottomed flan
dish. Trim the edges and reserve the
trimmings. Prick the pastry base
with a fork and refrigerate.
3 To make the filling: Put the syrup,
bread crumbs, lemon rind and juice
into a small saucepan and heat
gently, stirring, until the ingredients

are thoroughly combined. [!] Leave
to cool before spooning into the
prepared pastry case.
4 Roll out the reserved pastry
trimmings and cut into long, ¼-
inch wide strips. Use to decorate
the top of the tart in a lattice pattern,
moistening the ends of the lattice

strips and pressing them firmly
against the edge of the pastry case
so they do not come loose during
baking.
5 Bake in the oven for about 25
minutes or until the pastry is golden
and the filling is just set. Serve warm
or cold with cream or custard.

Cook's Notes

TIME
Preparation 20 minutes,
cooking time 25 minutes.

COOK'S TIPS
To measure the corn
syrup, first warm the
corn syrup container in a bowl
of hot water so that the syrup
flows freely. This is a traditional,
popular British recipe which is
normally made with golden
syrup, but sometimes black
treacle is used.

● 460 calories per portion

WATCHPOINT
Do not allow the mix-
ture to boil or it will re-
semble toffee.

VARIATION
Make tart on a 9-inch
pie plate and decorate
with a sunflower edge as shown
in the photograph: Cut the
pastry edge into 1-inch strips,
fold the strips diagonally in half
and press down firmly. Glaze
the edge by brushing with egg
yolk which has been beaten
with a little milk.

Banana fan flambé

SERVES 4

 4 large bananas, cut into fans (see Preparation)

 ¼ cup rum

juice of 1½ oranges

¼ teaspoon cinnamon

large pinch of freshly ground nutmeg

6 tablespoons butter

little lightly beaten egg white

4 tablespoons light brown sugar

vanilla ice cream or whipped cream, to serve

1 Pour the rum into a cup and stand in a pan or bowl of hot water to warm through gently. In a separate cup, mix the orange juice with the cinnamon and nutmeg.

2 Melt the butter in a large, heavy-bottomed skillet over low heat. Lightly brush fans with egg white, then add them to the pan and cook gently for about 5 minutes, turning once, until golden brown on both sides. ⚠ Sprinkle over the sugar.

3 Pour in the spiced orange juice and heat through gently. Turn off the heat. Pour the warmed rum over the bananas and immediately set light to it. ⚠ Let the flames die completely, then divide the fans and sauce between 4 warmed individual dishes and serve with ice cream.

Cook's Notes

TIME
Preparation and cooking take about 20 minutes.

 WATCHPOINTS
Use a spatula and turn the fans very gently so that they do not break or lose their attractive shape.

Hold the match just above the side of the pan and stand well back since the flames will shoot high for a few seconds and could be dangerous.

● 330 calories per portion

 PREPARATION
Make banana fans as follows:

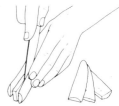

Cut each banana across in half. With a sharp knife, make 3-4 parallel cuts lengthwise in each half towards tapered end. Do not cut right through. Fan out slices.

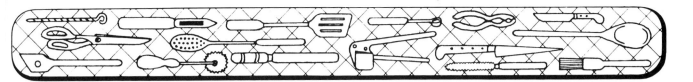

Gooseberry fool

SERVES 4

1 pint gooseberries, topped and
    tailed if fresh (see Preparation),
    thawed and well drained if frozen
    (see Watchpoints)
2 tablespoons water
¼ cup superfine sugar
2 cups vanilla pudding, cooled
few drops of green food coloring
⅔ cup plain yogurt
4 teaspoons colored sugar crystals
    (optional)

1 Put the gooseberries into a heavy-
bottomed saucepan with the water.
Cover and cook over moderate heat
for about 8 minutes, until soft.
2 Press the gooseberries through a
strainer, or cool slightly, then purée
in a blender and strain the purée to
remove seeds. Sweeten to taste with
superfine sugar, then leave to cool
completely.
3 Stir the purée into the pudding
until evenly blended, then add
enough coloring to tint the fool
pale green. Cover and refrigerate for
1-2 hours, if liked.
4 Divide the fool between 4 dessert
glasses or bowls. Spoon a little
yogurt carefully onto each portion.
5 Just before serving, scatter the
yogurt with sugar crystals if liked.
[!] Serve at room temperature or,
chilled.

Cook's Notes

 TIME
25 minutes preparation,
plus cooling and chill-
ing time.

 WATCHPOINT
If using thawed goose-
berries, drain them on
paper towels before cooking
otherwise the purée will be too
watery.
    Sugar crystals will dissolve if

added more than 5 minutes
before serving.

 SERVING IDEAS
This smooth, light des-
sert needs to be served
with crisp cookies for texture
contrast.

STORAGE
Prepare up to the end of
stage 3; cover with

plastic wrap and refrigerate for
up to 24 hours.

 PREPARATION
Use a small, sharp stain-
less steel knife to trim
off the small fibrous stalks and
"tails" from fresh gooseberries.
This is called "topping and
tailing."

● 200 calories per portion

Flaky rice sundae

SERVES 4

SERVES 4
2½ cups milk
½ cup flaked rice (see Buying
 guide)
2 tablespoons sugar
few drops of vanilla

TOPPING
1 tablespoon butter or margarine
1 tablespoon corn syrup
1 cup corn flakes or rice crispies

1 Pour the milk into a medium heavy-bottomed saucepan. Bring slowly to simmering point over low heat, then sprinkle in the flaked rice. Simmer gently, stirring frequently, for 15-20 minutes, until the rice is tender and thickened. [!]
2 Remove from the heat and stir in the sugar and vanilla, to taste. Cool slightly, then spoon into 4 dessert

dishes. Leave to cool completely.
3 Make the topping: Melt the butter with the syrup in a saucepan over low heat. Remove from the heat, add the corn flakes and stir

gently with a large metal spoon until evenly coated.
4 Spoon the topping over the sundaes. [!] Leave to set about 30 minutes before serving.

Cook's Notes

TIME
35 minutes preparation, plus cooling time.

BUYING GUIDE
You can buy white and brown rice flakes. The brown variety, which are sold in health food stores, have a pleasant "nutty" flavor and more food value.

! WATCHPOINTS
The milk should only simmer gently, otherwise it will evaporate and the pudding will be too thick.
The topping sticks together and hardens as it cools, so it

must be divided between the dishes while still warm.

SERVING IDEAS
This easy-to-make milk pudding with its tempting crisp, sweet topping can also be served hot. Spoon the pudding into the dishes, but do not cool; make and add the topping, then serve at once.

VARIATIONS
Try this topping over other milk puddings (canned, if liked), such as sago or semolina.

● 240 calories per portion

INDEX